GOWER

In memory of my father, Rowland
Nigel Jenkins

In memory of my mother, Irene
David Pearl

Published in 2009 by
Gomer Press, Llandysul, Ceredigion, SA44 4JL

ISBN 978 1 84851 052 4
A CIP record for this title is available from the British Library.

Design template: mopublications.com

This book is published with the financial support of the Welsh Books Council.

Printed and bound in Wales at
Gomer Press, Llandysul, Ceredigion

GOWER

NIGEL JENKINS & DAVID PEARL

CONTENTS

INTRODUCTION

The campaign to have Gower – too beautiful, perhaps, for its own good – designated Britain's first Area of Outstanding Natural Beauty[1] was driven by an awareness of the unprecedented pressures being exerted on the peninsula by urban encroachment and the mass tourism that burgeoned during the 'never had it so good' 1950s. AONB status, conferred in 1956, has helped protect Gower from all manner of developments – from the inappropriate to the monstrous – that have been proposed over the years; in the words of Vernon Watkins, the pre-eminent poet of Gower, its 'landscape survives, and [its] holy creatures proclaim their regenerate joys'.[2]

Gower has seen more alteration in the last one hundred years than during the previous five hundred. Born and raised in Gower, I have witnessed over half a century's worth of changes – not all of them, by any means, for the worse. Until the Second World War, the peninsula was a self-sufficient agricultural independency with its own dialect of English (and some Welsh on the north side) and institutions such as Courts Leet, the Mari Lwyd,[3] ploughing and hedging competitions, harvest suppers – and a resolutely conservative squirearchy that brooked no alteration in Gower's state.

The flavour of a way of life that is gone now forever is amply evoked in the folk poetry of Cyril Gwynn, bard of pre-war Gower, who anticipated some of the technological and demographic changes that would threaten the peninsula's integrity.[4] The town (Swansea) is a place of 'noise and riot' poised, in one of his prophetic dreams, to spill over into rural Gower, resulting in the despoliation of the countryside and the corrosion of social relationships. Until the mid 19th century, the peninsula's roads were so primitive that south Gower people had more dealings with Devon and Cornwall than with Swansea. Gower's relative inaccessibility nurtured in some an isolationist frame of mind that lingered well beyond the coming of motorised transport; as late as the 1950s, for instance, I remember

[1] By 2008, there were 40 AONBs in Wales and England.
[2] From 'Taliesin in Gower', in Vernon Watkins's *New Selected Poems*, Carcanet, 2006.
[3] Literally, 'Holy Mary': a form of wassailing involving a horse's skull.
[4] Although composed largely in the first half of the 20th century, the verse of Cyril Gwynn, published initially as *Gower Yarns* (1928) and subsequently, in an expanded edition, as *The Gower Yarns of Cyril Gwynn* (1976; edited for Gower Society publications by J. Mansel Thomas), remains popular; the latter volume, frequently reprinted, had sold 6,000 copies by 2009.

hearing of a woman in my home village of Parkmill who went to town so rarely that she missed out entirely on the era of the Swansea tram.

Increasing prosperity in the 1950s and an explosion in car ownership swept away the self-contained Gower of fond and no doubt rose-tinted memory. The peninsula's beaches, chief among them Oxwich, Port Eynon and Llangennith, became hugely popular weekend destinations for the newly mobile populations of towns such as Swansea, Llanelli and Cardiff. Not far behind the day-trippers came the campers and caravanners from all over Britain, who would become for many a farmer a much more lucrative 'crop' than mere potatoes or mangolds. With some 18 million people living within a four-hour drive of Gower, the peninsula's resident population of 10,000 may be swollen by 50,000 day-trippers on a sunny Saturday or Sunday, in addition to the 30,000 holidaymakers pitched here for a week or more. Some well-heeled 'discoverers' of this 'hidden gem' have returned to its shores to buy a holiday home or retirement nest, and the bourgeoisie of Swansea (and elsewhere) have not been slow to jump on the property bandwagon, paying half a million or more for the ownership of a spectacular Gower view.

The landscape, indeed, survives. From the back seat of a four-by-four bundling across Fairwood Common laden with groceries purchased hundreds of miles away, Gower may seem a comfortingly unchanging place. The consumers of scenery are unlikely, however, to want to trouble their heads with the break-up of farms, rural unemployment, natives priced out of the housing market, the closure of village shops and post offices, overburdened natural habitats, the creeping amnesia of suburbanisation – afflictions all too familiar, of course, in other famously beautiful parts of Britain. It's as well to be aware of such developments (and of the poet Harri Webb's excoriation of 'this beauty that is meaningless, / That's bought and sold on every side'),[5] the better to raise a constructively critical voice, but not to be so oppressed by them that we lose sight of our extraordinary good fortune in being able to live in or visit what remains a uniquely magnetic corner of Wales.

A word or two by way of orientation . . . It is not, please note, 'the Gower', common as that misnomer may be, but either 'the Gower peninsula' or plain 'Gower'. Quite how that erroneous usage developed is unclear. It has been suggested that when the people of the southern coalfield were largely Welsh-speaking they would refer to the Vale of

[5] From 'Thoughts in an Area of Outstanding Natural Beauty' in Harri Webb's *A Crown for Branwen*, Gomer Press, 1974.

Glamorgan/Bro Morgannwg as 'Y Fro' (The Vale), and that when they began making excursions to Gower they tagged an habitual 'Y' onto the peninsula, rendering it 'Y Gŵyr' (The Gower). It has never been known in Welsh as 'Y Gŵyr', but simply 'Gŵyr' – and that, unencumbered by a direct article in either language, is how Gower folk tend to like it.

Another much neglected point is that the 188 sq. km peninsula, with its 64 km of coastline and its 19 bays, comprises only half the picture. Gower, in the full sense, is roughly commensurate with the ancient commote of Gŵyr which, following the Norman conquest of Gower in the early 1100s, became the lordship of Gower, with its *caput* at Swansea. There is a 'Gower of the Hills' – bounded by the Llwchwr, the Aman, the Twrch and the Tawe – which reaches as far inland, in a north-easterly direction, as the peninsula prows into the Severn Sea. This is Gower *Wallicana* (Welsh Gower) where thousands still speak the language that the conquerors so efficiently 'cleansed' from Gower *Anglicana* (English Gower), and whose communities were part of the coal, steel and tinplate world of the southern valleys. The region is dominated by high and majestic moorlands, and its inhabitants have recently been involved in an heroic struggle to prevent cash generators – promoted as wind turbines – from disfiguring some of its loveliest wildernesses. They have argued that the AONB should be extended to embrace Gower *Wallicana*; others have proposed that all of Gower, from the Aman to Worms Head, should become Wales's fourth National Park. The whole of historic Gower, which belonged by geography and culture to south-west Wales until forced into Glamorgan by the 1536 Act of 'Union', still has a unified existence as the parliamentary constituency of Gower, which was established in 1918. And, more by accident than design, the confines of the ancient commote of Gŵyr are roughly those of the modern City and County of Swansea.

It has been a pleasure to collaborate in the making of this book with my friend David Pearl, who has worked with me on various photographic, book-design and glass art-work projects in the past (he is a glass artist with an international reputation). Born to Welsh and English parents and raised in Canada, David is nevertheless an old Gower hand, having lived in Swansea since the mid 1970s. For his stimulating company on many a Gower ramble and for his superb photographs I am warmly grateful.

****

FARMS

Cocklebushes, Deer Park, The Lawn, Six Acres, Poppins Park, The Leg . . . Just an odd list of names; but to me, these field names are among the most resonantly evocative and poignant words I know. To dwell on them is to conjure from the drizzles of forgetfulness both a green-and-golden childhood and a farm not untypical of the dozens of Gower farms which in recent decades have been blown chaff-like into oblivion by 'market forces'.

If it's true that you are not fully dead until your name has been spoken on earth for the very last time, then the ability of the remaining survivors of Kilvrough Park Farm (my brother, my sister, my mother and me) to name all its fields assures the old farm, for a few years more, of a spectral existence in our imaginations. But, having been sold off piecemeal, like so many others, the farm now has half a dozen different owners, not one of whom is likely to know the names of the few fields he owns, let alone the names of neighbouring plots, all of which once cohered, under a single family's ownership, as 148 acres of prime agricultural land, with a history, a personality, a culture. As a farm divested of its names, its unity and all productive purpose, the place no longer makes sense. All that's produced here are appearances: the vague *look* of a farm; a field striped by chain harrows to resemble a suburban lawn; the conspicuously indulgent trappings of 'horsiculture'. And to look like a bit of a farmer because you've bought a field or two and a barn or a shed, would seem to be enough to entitle you to build a house on your 'farm' – which has been for many a nifty circumvention of the AONB's supposedly stringent planning regulations. Where once there was a single farmhouse in the midst of a working farm, there may now be a rash of 'farmhouses' – of boxy or grandiloquently pretentious design, with rootless names, pseudo-Victorian lamp posts and defensive electric gates – dotting the pathetically redundant fields.

Kilvrough's situation is far from unique. In an area of roughly 2 sq. km – bounded by Southgate and Parkmill to the west, Fairwood Common to the north, Bishopston to the

east, and the coast to the south – there once thrived, until well into the 1970s, at least a dozen farms, in addition to the twenty market gardens of Bishopston. The market gardens long ago disappeared, and there are now only two or three fully functioning farms. The rest have been sold off in dribs and drabs – a field here, two fields there – as incomes have diminished, debts have mounted and younger generations have forsaken the land for a better living elsewhere (myself, *mea culpa*, among them). It's a pattern repeated throughout Gower: by 2008, there were fewer than ten dairy farms left in the entire peninsula, and only about four farms growing the famed Gower potato. My brother Martyn, who enjoys a much higher standard of living as an agricultural valuer than he could have achieved as a farmer, says he hasn't sold a whole farm in Gower for years: 'When a farmer decides to call it a day, he knows that market conditions determine that he'll get a far better deal for himself by selling his land off in bits and pieces – even though, sadly, that will mean the end of the farm as a going concern. I can't see that there will ever be a way of putting these pieces back together again to make viable farms.'

It was the quality of its farmland that first attracted the Normans to south Gower – its loamy brown-earth soils, its well-drained limestone base, its favourable and relatively frost-free climate; and there remain one or two names on the home patch which can be read as bitter souvenirs of the invaders' drive to wrest the land out of Welsh hands and to resist native attempts to regain control. One of the few Welsh place names in the parish of Pennard is that of a ruined farmhouse, Pwll-y-bloggi (resort of the wolf dog), which would seem to record a battle against the Normans on 15 April, 1136, after which packs of wolves descended from the hills to feast on the bodies of the 516 men killed in the conflict. Then there is that curious name, Kilvrough. My parents used to joke that it meant 'the abode of swine', which I took to be a groundless fancy until the poet Harri Webb (1920–94) suggested to me that Kilvrough could well be an Anglicisation of *cil-yr-hwch* (retreat of the sow) – the sow being none other than Llywelyn Fawr (Llywelyn ap Iorwerth, Prince of Wales; *c.*1173–1240), known hereabouts for the swinish ferocity with which he and his warriors would rout up everything that stood in their path.

But it was the invaders who prevailed, consigning the natives to the heavy, damp, acid soils of the north and north-east, and establishing in the south, around nucleated villages, their manorial system of open fields, divided into strips of an acre or more. The clifftop walk between Rhosili village and the tip of the headland passes alongside a substantial tract known as the Vile (or Vyle or Viel),[1] which retains to this day its medieval open-field layout, with the strips – up to about 40 m wide – bounded by low grassy banks known as landshares. Each strip, intended to be as large as a man could plough in one day, has a name, such as Sandyland, Priest Hay and Bramble Bush. Bishopston too was known for small, elongated fields fashioned originally by the Normans.

While the clifftops and commons provided ample grazing for sheep and cattle, the fields were used largely for cultivation. Given the relatively limited dimensions of the peninsula – 20 km long and no more than 10 km wide – Gower's farms have been capable of much greater variety than nearby areas. The uplands of Glamorgan, for instance, have been confined largely to sheep rearing, while southern Carmarthenshire has been known mainly for dairying. But all seven main types of farming have been possible in Gower: sheep, dairying, beef and mixed livestock, pigs and poultry, cropping, horticulture and – the most common of all – mixed, a sustainable system that endured for centuries.

Most of Gower's open fields, as those elsewhere, underwent enclosure in the 18th century. They were worked, particularly in south Gower, largely by tenant farmers who paid their dues to the big estate owners, chief among them the Talbots of Penrice, the Lucases of Stouthall, and the Dawkinses (and subsequently the Penrices and Lyonses) of Kilvrough. The demise of the big estates, a process which began with the break-up of Kilvrough in 1919 and ended with the sale of Clyne and Parc le Breos in the 1950s, represented a liberation for the peninsula's tenant farmers. Many bought their farms at highly favourable rates and most were relieved that they were no longer answerable to representatives of a sometimes autocratic *ancien régime*. Becoming surer of their future, many farmers grew land-hungry; their expansionism introduced an element of fluidity in land boundaries which, for generations, had remained the same.

The dispersal of the 4,000-acre Kilvrough Estate gave my grandfather, T.E. (Tom) Jenkins, who had been the Lyonses' agent, the opportunity to acquire two neighbouring farms. With a loan of £8,000, he bought the estate's home farm, Kilvrough Farm, opposite Kilvrough Manor, and Kilvrough Park Farm on the other side of the road (the A4118 south

plough and tractor
mobbed by gulls; the sheen
of bladed earth

in anchored flight
from the barbed fence –
spider-lines, horsehair

[1] This is often said to be the old Gower rendition of 'field', but it may be derived from *vill*, an Old French word for 'feudal township', in which case Vile/Viel may mean something like 'land belonging to the village [of Rhosili]'. It is possible that because there was a monastic settlement at Rhosili prior to the Norman conquest the fields may be of pre-Norman origin.

Gower road) – which, the family having eventually sold Kilvrough Farm, was where my brother, my sister and I were raised.

My grandfather began his farming life during a period of considerable change. New varieties of grasses were being experimented with, and potato growing and mixed farming burgeoned. The advent of mechanized transport in 1922 enabled the easy and rapid transit of crops and livestock to markets in Swansea and further afield. The installation of piped water supplies encouraged increased milk production. The mid 1930s saw the first Fordson tractors arriving in Gower, while the government introduced the first in a long series of measures to subsidize agricultural production, lending a degree of security to a way of life which for centuries had been hard and precarious.

Ours was a typical mixed farm. We had a herd of about twenty milking cows and twenty or so beef cattle, a small flock of sheep, half a dozen pigs, some chickens, a few ducks and sometimes geese. We grew hay, barley, oats, wheat, potatoes, swedes, mangolds (for feeding the cattle) and, in a kitchen garden, beans, peas, cabbages, sprouts and salad vegetables, largely for our own consumption. We shot pigeons, rabbits and the odd hare. The rationing imposed during the Second World War continued well into the 1950s, but we were hardly aware of it, because, like most other Gower farming families at that time, we were more or less self-sufficient in food.

Farming, of this traditional kind, represented not just a living but a way of life. The farm whose recent fragmentation has rendered it meaningless was once fecund with meaning. It nourished our present, proposed a future, and connected us, in disparate ways, with a sense of the past which encompassed elements ranging from intimately personal stories to narratives seeded by such far-flung places as India and Abyssinia. Bounded by three roads and a wooded ridge, it formed, roughly, a square patch of fields, akin to the *milltir sgwâr*, the cosily familiar 'square mile' of Welsh rural tradition, set within the wider home locality of the *bro*, which embraced neighbouring farms and nearby villages.

In the corner of the farm's south-easternmost field, Church Park, is the (possibly) 14th-century Pennard Church, where the family were christened, married and buried, and where the few believers among us regularly worshipped, while the rest ignored the tolling across our fields of the church's mournful bell. Harri Webb is buried here, and there's a plaque

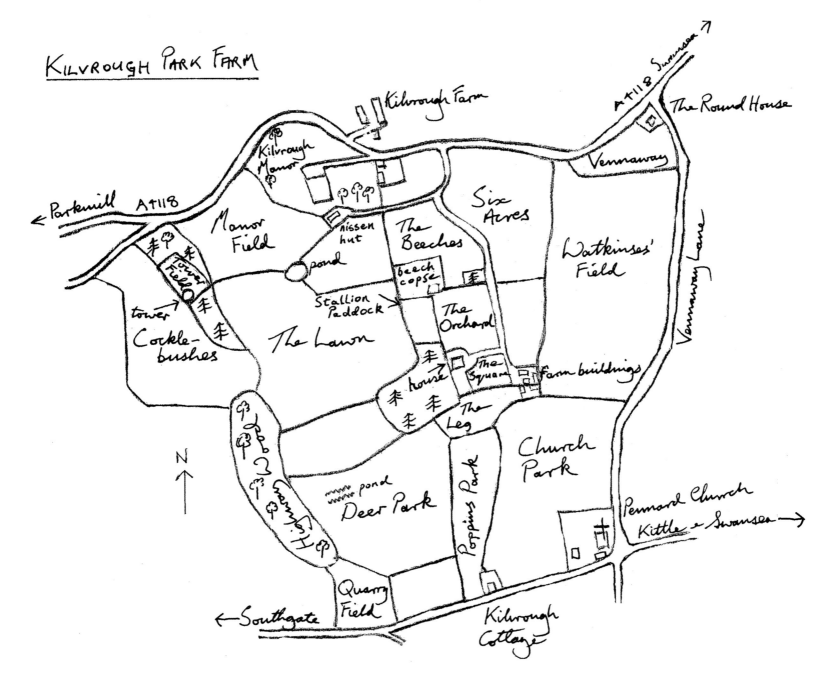

KILVROUGH PARK FARM

Kilvrough Farm

The Round House

A+118 Swansea

Venmaway

Kilvrough Manor

Six Acres

Watkinses' Field

←Parkmill A+118

Manor Field

nissen hut

The Beeches

beech copse

pond

Stallion Paddock

tower

Tower Field

The Lawn

The Orchard

Cockle-bushes

house

The Square

Farm buildings

The Leg

Venmaway Lane

N

Highmoor

pond

Deer Park

Poppins Park

Church Park

Pennard Church

Kittle & Swansea →

Quarry Field

←Southgate

Kilvrough Cottage

15

'beware', says the sign
at the churchyard gate,
'of unsafe gravestones'

inside the church commemorating the poet Vernon Watkins (1906–1967) who lived on the cliffs at Pennard and worshipped in this church.

A few hundred metres west of the church, and at the southern end of Poppins Park, was Kilvrough Cottage – now extended and uPVC-ed out of recognition – where my paternal great-grandfather lived. I still have the remains of the pocket watch that the widowed and dilapidated old farmer used to take to pieces, and dreamily shove back together again, to pass the time in his last long days.

At the farm's south-westernmost point was an area of Deer Park known as Quarry Field, after the small, disused quarry that lurked beneath a fringe of scrubby trees. What buildings of limestone were quarried for here, I have often wondered – the church, the farm's cowshed, our house, with the date of its construction, 1886, over the porch?

At the north-western edge of our 'square world' was Kilvrough Manor, a youth hostel in the 1950s and now an outward-bound centre owned by Oxfordshire Education Committee, but formerly the manorial hub of a great Gower estate, and a player in events of high drama and some exoticism. It was from here that Major Thomas Penrice, the squire of Kilvrough, led about thirty men of the Swansea and Fairwood Corps of Yeomen Cavalry to engage, somewhat ineffectually, with the armed insurrectionists of Merthyr Tydfil, during the Merthyr Rising of 1831; the major and his men seem to have spent much of the encounter in a pub at Aberpergwm. And then there was the visit to Kilvrough of the Emperor of Abyssinia, Haile Selassie, descendant of King Solomon and the Queen of Sheba, and the black messiah of the Rastafarian faith. My grandmother remembered meeting the emperor there, perhaps when his son, Prince Lidi Asrate Kasa, was a pupil at the Bible College School, Blackpill, during the early years of the Second World War. She also handed on the story of an attempt, in 1809, to commit suttee at the manor, by the part-Indian widow of another military owner of Kilvrough, Major William Crompton Green of the East India Company. Following Major Green's death, his distraught widow was determined to burn herself alive along with the body of her husband on a funeral pyre on the lawn, in accordance with Hindu custom. Mrs Green's proposal horrified the locals, and it was only by the most strenuous exertions that she was persuaded against self-immolation, eventually allowing her husband to be buried in Pennard churchyard.

the stripped elm,
after the storm,
shimmering with sun-shot
buds of rain

It's clear from any map that the main south Gower road used to go straight past the front door of Kilvrough Manor, but when the estate was being freshly landscaped in the 18th century the road was diverted in a dramatic loop to the north. Its teetering wall – the bane of motorists unused to Gower's wayward roads – is topped with triangular coping blocks cast from copper slag produced at the Vivians' Hafod (Swansea) copper works.

The same kind of blue-black blocks of slag top the garden wall of the Round House at the farm's north-easterly corner. My grandmother, who lived here for many years, used to explain that an earlier version of the house was indeed round.[2] It had been built in about 1840 to control a turnpike toll gate – of the kind which so affronted the hard-pressed small farmers of south-west Wales that, as the Daughters of Rebecca, they rose against their oppressors, attacking the hated toll gates, at which they had been obliged to pay extortionate fees, and ultimately forcing the abolition of the turnpike trusts which profited from the tolls. In 1843, Rebecca had 'visited' and entirely destroyed the Pound-ffald toll gate in Three Crosses a couple of miles away. They were thought to have the Kilvrough toll gate in their sights, and special constables were deployed at the Round House, but there were no further Rebecca visitations in Gower.

Some of the fields' names – Cocklebushes, Poppins Park – defy explanation, although, for me, they are as evocative of the acres they describe as is the 'abstract' name of a dear friend.

Some are self-explanatory: the high-walled and stoutly hedged Stallion Paddock; or The Orchard, with a meagre scattering of aged apple and pear trees where once there would have been scores in carefully tended rows. (Gower was once renowned for its orchards.) Many names probably originated during the period of busy field creation inaugurated by the enclosure acts of the 18th century, and several – The Lawn, Deer Park – characterize the artfully planned parkland so beloved of the 18th- and 19th-century gentry. In the walled Tower Field, where we kept pigs (and where, in 2008, pigs were again being raised), there was a classic parkland folly, a circular tower which had once had two storeys, but was now open to the sky, its flooring long decayed. As a romantic teenager, I used to fantasize (with W.B. Yeats in mind) about restoring the tower and secluding myself there – with wine, books and a beautiful girl – to compose poetry.

[2] An alternative explanation which I later heard is that it was named after a circular animal pound opposite, which is no longer extant.

One poem I wanted to write – and have yet to do so – concerned the white owl which used to roost in the tower, and which used to fascinate my infant father when his mother took him on walks there. They would find the owl perched asleep on a ledge just below the tower's battlemented rim. One day they stumbled on the owl lying dead in nearby Highway Wood; someone had shot it.

The Second World War made its mark. The manor was used as a billet for troops, and one or two asbestos Nissen huts were erected on the farm, perhaps in connection with the aerodrome that was constructed, in some desperation, on Fairwood Common in 1941. One of these huts, tucked in behind the manor, was later the home of the cowman and his family, and I lived there myself for some years in the 1970s.

The concrete base of another was to be found in a corner of Church Park. Until the aerodrome was completed, there was a landing strip on what we called Watkinses' fields – after the Watkins family of Widegate, who rented the land from us. Those fields must have had older names, but clearly they were lost during our tenure of the farm, thanks to our carelessness – just as the remaining names that were transmitted to us down the generations are unknown to the land's latest owners. Cocklebushes, for instance, has become the Gower Riding Club Field. The entire farm, bereft of its traditional names and of all familial and historic associations, could be renamed Terra Incognita.

I walked the old farm guiltily one recent summer's day – the guilt occasioned not by my trespassing but by the uncomfortable recognition that my abdication, as a fugitive teenager, of what could have been a birthright had played no small part in the farm's eventual demise. The mewing in this wilderness of a lone buzzard provided a mournful accompaniment as I tramped through ungrazed thicknesses of grass, and struggled in vain – through swathes of shoulder-high nettle, thistle and bramble pushing deep into the fields from untended hedgerows – to find old gateways into the woods, which were now unmanaged, impenetrable jungles. Familiar lines of connection from field to (clogged) pond to woodland path were obstructed at every turn by the barbed-wired, wasteful untidiness of it all. The place was like an abandoned student flat in which no one had washed any dishes for years.

DAUGHTERS

A halt on the turn
to roll himself a smoke,
the forgotten crows
clattering back to mind
as the tractor drops throttle.

Do ponies remember?
He steps to the gate, and she
steps to meet him, cracked hooves
trailing dead winter couch.
For them, now,
in their mother's furs, out with
boys every night –
she no longer exists.

And he no longer
need break from ploughing or
carrying hay
to coax a bit between
her teeth and girth her up tight
with his strong hands.

He has bred, they have eaten:
the bedroom is wide
on a clutter of lipsticks,
greasepots and shoes,
cigarette smoke leaving
by a vent in the wall.

Back then to the tractor. One
jerk at the throttle
obliterates crows, sends him
hurtling down the headland
out of one more winter
to another spring.

the hedge-layer's pyre –
swirled round in its waning
by an onrush of snow . . .

in from dusk to
a house still warm with day's heat,
the bloom of wild garlic

There are similar ghost farms throughout the peninsula. Like farmers elsewhere in Wales, those of Gower have had to contend with a seemingly limitless onslaught of impediments and disincentives, from the crises of BSE ('mad cow disease'), foot-and-mouth disease, bovine tuberculosis and various food scares, to tidal waves of form-filling and bureaucracy, and the crippling expense of items such as machinery, chemical fertilizers and fuel. Most farmers work more than sixty hours a week, yet incomes have fallen by over fifty per cent since 1995: all too often, they end up selling the food they produce for less than it costs them to produce it. Fifty cows would once have been considered a sizeable herd, but these days – with supermarket milk being cheaper than bottled water – the dairy farmer needs about 300 milkers to have a chance of survival. Then there's globalisation: the capitalist madness (and rank immorality) of using virtual slave labour in 'developing' countries to rear poor quality animals (and other foodstuffs), in conditions that would be illegal here, for meat that is shipped halfway round the world and sold to us overfed dupes at knock-down prices in Tesco – while thousands of children in those countries die every day of starvation and malnutrition.

No human activity is more important than the production of food. Although life for most Gower farmers has never been easy, they worked their land resourcefully for centuries, to produce not only an abundance of food but a society and a culture, both of which have been in serious decline for decades. With the ending of automatic subsidies after 2013, the future for agriculture has never looked more uncertain. The ruination of Gower's farms seems doomed to continue, and for many there would seem to be no alternative. But sooner or later, it seems to me, the worsening global food crisis will reach such a desperate pitch as to enforce – let's hope without recourse to military coercion – the social ownership of productive land: for the production, once again, of the staple of life.

****

THE VIEW FROM CEFN BRYN

There's no better way of encompassing the lie of Gower's land than walking the peninsula's *massif central*, the 6.5-km whaleback ridge of Cefn Bryn.

Many begin this walk at Penmaen church, but to take the full measure of Cefn Bryn (back + hill) I like to start at Parkmill, at more or less sea level, and meander upwards along the old packhorse 'road'. Opposite the sprawling heritage centre, you peel away from the busy 'new' road (the A4118) shortly after the bridge over the Green Cwm stream. There's a fine view of Pennard Castle to your left, just before you're enveloped by the tall beech and ash trees that flank this ancient thoroughfare. Never a route for wheeled vehicles, the trackway is a rugged reminder of how slow and arduous overland journeys used to be before road improvements were made in the middle of the 19th century; until then, the sea having provided the most efficient means of transportation for centuries, Gower farmers and quarrymen did more trade with Cornwall than they did with Swansea. It wasn't until further improvements in the 1920s that motorised vehicles could negotiate the peninsula's roads.

After a few hundred metres, the old road – hemmed in now by thick hedges – swings south, between fields on either side, and the going gets gentler as the incline shallows. As you approach North Hills Farm, with Cefn Bryn rearing invitingly ahead, it's worth cutting across the neat campsite on your left to take in one of Britain's most popular picture-postcard views (some call it iconic, others a cliché): the triple-peaked and cave-holed limestone peninsula that gives Three Cliffs Bay its name, with the Pennard Pill flowing sinuously around it. To the west of the beach is a spit of sand dunes, much reduced in recent decades, where Gower's most short-lived 'castle' stood for a week or so in 1959, during the filming of a big-budget movie called *The Inspector*. Made of hardboard and accompanied by a few fake palm trees, the set turned Three Cliffs into a Palestinian beach – at the same time as it neatly obscured from camera the shacks on the hillside behind. The beach was 'invaded' by a Comet tank, which left tracks in the marsh that were visible for years.

By this juncture, the rough old 'road' has become an asphalted lane, with the barns and sheds of North Hills Farm on your right converted to (dung-free) tourist accommodation (note here a length of characteristic estate wall, topped with triangular slag blocks from the Hafod copper works), and, to your left, a row of houses leading to the junction with the main south Gower road, from which you diverged in Parkmill. Crossing the road, you might dip into the heavily 'restored' (that is, virtually rebuilt) Penmaen church to peruse a tombstone, set in the north wall of the chancel, which is a notably flamboyant example, in English, of Welsh pedigree boasting – with the traditional 'ap' being replaced here by 'the sonne of'. The tombstone, dated 1623, traces the deceased's ancestry back a further ten generations, to culminate royally in Iestyn ap Gwrgant (fl. 1081–1100), king of Glamorgan:

> Here resteth the body of David the sonne of David the sonne of Richard the sonne of Nicholas the sonne of Rys the sonne of Leison the sonne of Rys the sonne of Morgan Ychan the sonne of Morgan the sonne of Cradock the sonne of Iustin ap Gwrgan Sometime Lord of Glamorgan . . .

Royalty of a different kind, a people's prince of song, is associated with the nearby old people's home of Glan-y-Mor (1861 and 1939; or Three Cliffs Residential Home, as it has become), the imposing complex (with its unfortunately portentous smokestack) to your left as you begin the final ascent of the Bryn. Phil Tanner (1862–1950), born of a family of Gower weavers famous in Llangennith for singing and dancing, spent his last nine years at Glan-y-Mor (or The Workhouse,[1] as it's sometimes remembered). It wasn't until 1937 that Phil's singing was recorded, and it was during his time at Glan-y-Mor that his fame – as the 'Gower nightingale' – spread beyond the home patch. He has long been acknowledged worldwide as one of the finest traditional singers in the English language.[2]

From here to the summit ridge takes only a few minutes, on a track – which continues most of the way to Reynoldston – once known as Talbot's Way, after Christopher Rice Mansel Talbot (1803–1890), of Penrice Castle, who used the route to ride with his hounds to his favourite hunting grounds at Parc le Breos. One of his daughters, Emily (1840–1918)

---

[1] It was built as a workhouse for fifty inmates, following the introduction of a new Gower Poor Law in 1857.
[2] A CD recording of eighteen of his songs, a tiny fraction of his (largely unrecorded) repertoire, along with an introductory broadcast by Wynford Vaughan Thomas, was released on the Veteran label in 2003 (VT145CD).

– who on her father's death became the richest heiress in Britain – had the track turfed for the benefit of riders, but the springy legacy of Miss Talbot (as she was always known) has long since given way to a quartzy underlay of rubbled sandstone. The Talbots and their descendants were a conservative force to be reckoned with, content to maintain Gower more or less as it had been for hundreds of years. In 1938, for instance, when a string of electricity poles was erected along Talbot's Way, Lady Blythswood (1870-1958), who had succeeded Miss Talbot as *châtelaine*, ordered the poles' immediate removal from the skyline.

If Benjamin Heath Malkin's 19th-century description of Cefn Bryn as 'a mountain, one of the highest in South Wales' was somewhat overblown, the Bryn is, nevertheless, at 186 m, the peninsula's second highest point, surpassed only by the Beacon on Rhosili Down at 197 m. And had Malkin visited 'Gower' about 300 million years ago, during the period of mountain creation caused by the slow violence of continents colliding, he would certainly have found a mountain: Cefn Bryn at that time was nearly 5,000 m high – higher than any mountain in modern western Europe, Mont Blanc (4,808 m) included. Since then, an astonishing 4,500 m or more of rock have been eroded from Cefn Bryn by the action of wind and water, aided by glaciation, plant roots and chemical degradation.

Although much tamed over the aeons, the Bryn can be a cold and forbiddingly windy place. I doubt that I have ever been so chilled to the marrow as when, one winter's day in the 1950s, my father took his two shivering boys for a ride on their shaggy ponies the length of Cefn Bryn, to call on friends in Reynoldston. By the time we reached their house, my unthinking faith in the Divine Right and Wisdom of Parents had been fatally undermined, and my frozen brother and I insisted on a car ride home. Even on a fine June day, there can be an insistent sea breeze fretting the pale wispy grasses and sending broken waves through the earthily aromatic bracken.

One of the most primitive forms of plant life, bracken has survived for some 300 million years by total domination of its habitat, the density of its cover stifling all other contenders. If the bracken in summer obscures many of the hill's archaeological sites, the Bryn is an ideal vantage point, at any time of the year, for grasping the basic geology of Gower. Two features are immediately apparent.

Firstly, there's the similar altitude (an average of 185 m) of the peninsula's highest ridges (Cefn Bryn, Llanmadoc Hill,[3] Rhosili Down), which consist of Devonian Red Sandstone, Gower's oldest rock. These monadnocks, eroded relics of an extensive wave-cut platform, are composed of sedimentary rocks, studded with pebbles of jasper and quartz; they were deposited about 400 million years ago, when the land that would become Wales was part of a monsoonal landmass that straddled the equator and was submerged for much of the time by huge, meandering river-systems. At other times, Cefn Bryn and its siblings would have protruded from the sea as islands – as doubtless they will again, at some point in a globally over-heated future.

Secondly, over 100 m lower than the sandstone ridges, there's the extensive plateau of Carboniferous Limestone – composed of an unimaginable accumulation of sea shells and fish bones, deposited to a depth of over 800 m about 350 million years ago: south Gower's planed and levelled headlands and clifftops, from Mumbles to Worms Head, are the plateau's most obvious manifestation.

The covered reservoir on Cefn Bryn dating from the early 1950s, which stores water pumped up from the Green Cwm stream, stands a couple of metres proud of the ridge. Although stoutly fenced, there's no lock on the gate – on the summer afternoon that David Pearl and I walk the Bryn – and nothing to prevent us ascending to its grassed-over 'lid' and treating ourselves to a remarkable panorama. Due north, across the Burry Inlet, there are Llanelli and the Trostre tinplate works, the last in Britain; then, panning eastward, and looking further inland, the wedgy scarp above Llyn y Fan Fach (48 km), Fan Gihirych (48 km) and the Brecon Beacons (60 km); due east, there are Swansea and Kilvey Hill (22 km), the smoke- and flame-gusting stacks of the steelworks at Port Talbot (26 km; named, of course, after the industrialist and land-rich Talbots of Penrice and Margam), Porthcawl (30 km) and Nash Point (43 km); south, across the Severn Sea, there are Exmoor (53 km), Ilfracombe (42 km), Hartland Point (69 km) and the island of Lundy (61 km).

Due west, across a snatch of Carmarthen Bay, which fills the dip between Hardings Down and Llanmadoc Hill, there's the faint gleam of the bright frontages of Tenby (37 km); to the north-west, there are Pendine (32 km), Laugharne (29 km), the golden miles of Cefn

copper shafts

through bundling grey, beaming up

the Severn Sea

---

[3] Known locally as Penny Hill, because it's sandwiched between the King's Head at Llangennith and the Britannia at Llanmadoc.

Sidan (19 km), and, in the misty distance, the hallowed heights of Preseli (58 km), a range as potent with cairn, standing stone and cromlech as this realm of Cefn Bryn, to which Preseli seems to call.

At our feet, in all directions, spreads Gower: we couldn't be standing in a more central position. With the exception of the beaches, the commons, the fenland at Oxwich and the vast saltmarsh of the northern seaboard, this is unmistakably an agricultural landscape, shaped by the minds and hands of farmers since the arrival in Gower of the first Neolithic (or New Stone Age) people about 6000 years ago. These pioneers of mixed farming relentlessly pursued the felling of the thick oakwood that had established itself since the end of the last ice age *c.* 11,500 BC, replacing the woodland with a patchwork of small, enclosed fields – not dissimilar to the patchwork, of all imaginable shades of green, that we see on either side of Cefn Bryn today. The most enduring traces of Gower's earliest farmers are the great cromlechs and burial chambers that are striking presences in the modern landscape, such as Sweyn's Houses on Rhosili Down, Giant's Grave in the Green Cwm, and – most famous of them all – Arthur's Stone on the north-western shoulder of the Bryn.

The hill had probably been cleared of trees by the beginning of the Bronze Age (*c.* 2,300 BC), as implied by the many barrows and cairns[4] that line its ridge and dot its slopes. The dense bracken makes them difficult to find in summer, but there is an extraordinary concentration of about 70 burial mounds on Cefn Bryn, suggesting that this ridge – like the Preselis – was unusually significant in the rites and mysteries of prehistoric peoples. Another characteristic Bronze Age relic, the standing stone, is also represented with rare intensity within the spiritually magnetic field of Cefn Bryn: in an area of 7 sq. kms in the parish of Llanrhidian about 10 monoliths have been identified. The place still casts an ineluctable spell, not least at night: wanting to escape from the light pollution of the city – the cupola of phosphorescence that 'protects' us from the dark – I have often come to Cefn Bryn to lie in my duffle coat on a bed of heather and to gaze up at the Milky Way, the ragged ribbon of 200,000 million suns that is our galactic home . . . as humbling and empowering an experience as it must have been for the Bronze Age farmers who sought transcendence here thousands of years ago.

frosty bark
as I squint the Pleiades
of fox, cadno, fox, fox

[4] Burial mounds predominantly of earth and stones respectively.

Water must have had something to do with the mystical significance of Cefn Bryn. There are dozens of springs flowing from its sides, many of them providing local people with this essential – and in former times, properly revered – life-source until the relatively recent advent of piped water supplies. The older houses along the south side of the Bryn owe their situation to the proximity of wells sunk into these springs, and several springs, particularly on the north side, have long had sacred associations: one such, Holy Well – to the south of the Cilibion–Reynoldston road where it rises towards the crest – was enclosed by the water authority to augment Gower's water supply.

The tree clearances pursued so industriously by Gower's early farmers had disastrous results, in some areas, when combined with a relentless deterioration in climate after 1,400 BC. Mean temperatures fell by almost two degrees centigrade; without tree cover to effect transpiration, increased rainfall led to waterlogging, the acidification of soil and the stifling by peat of formerly productive hillside acres – which dovetailed here with the huge tract of moor and bog stretching north from Cefn Bryn towards the fields around Llanrhidian, with here and there a stunted alder and, in high summer, patches of cotton-grass like unseasonal dustings of snow.

Human activity in this 'green desert' is concentrated these days on the busy Cilibion–Reynoldston road, which, before it was asphalted, used to be known as the Red Road, after its red sandstone base; it was also known as the Coal Road, as this was the route taken by carts delivering coal to western Gower from the peninsula's coal-mining belt along the northern coast from Wernffrwd to Gowerton. Just west of Cilibion, the road skirts one of Gower's relatively few freshwater lakes, Broad Pool – although 'lake' might be accounted a Malkinesque exaggeration, as it's little more than a hectare in area and only chest-high at its deepest. Once or twice a century, it dries out, as it did in the drought of 1984 – which made it possible to dredge the 2000 tonnes of silt and plant material that were clogging up the pool and threatening to turn it into a bog.

Looking north beyond Broad Pool, an altogether vaster experience of water is conveyed by the Burry Inlet, which is also the estuary of the river Llwchwr, and a wetland of world importance. At high tide, the whole inlet, saltmarshes and all, is inundated by the sea, but no less a sensation of immense space is evoked by the scene at low tide, especially on days of hurtling cloud, when a patch of sunlight, having highlighted a rectangle of lemony hayfield, will seconds later ignite a swathe of exposed sandbank before illuminating the mudflats and sparking across the Llwchwr's sluggish path in the direction of Llanelli. There was a time, before a channel was dredged up to Llanelli, when it was possible to cross the inlet by foot or on horseback: John Wesley recorded doing so in 1764.

Having granted us glimpses of the Bronze Age, the view also opens a window on the Iron Age (*c*. 750 BC–AD 50) that succeeded it (and through which, in many ways, we are still living today). Beyond Broad Pool and in profile against the Burry Inlet, there's the 118-m Cilifor Top, its millstone-grit summit crowned slantwise by the diminished and grassed-over remains of huge ramparts and ditches. Constructed *c.*100 BC, this 3-ha Iron Age hillfort is an impressive example of the many defensive earthworks thrown up in Gower by the warrior Celts, indelibly stamping their presence on the landscape.

Little is known of Roman activities in the peninsula, and even less of those of the Vikings. But it is generally assumed that the indigenous people managed to hold their own until the coming of the Vikings' land-ravenous continental cousins, the Normans, in the late 10th century. What happened then – the forcible occupation of Gower's best farmland in the sun-facing south and the banishment of the natives to the poorer, acid soils of the north and north-east – is inscribed in the landscape to this day. In the relatively thin belt of productive land to the north of Cefn Bryn, the fields and the farms are smaller; hemmed in by huge tracts of boggy common and marsh, the mood is one of prudence and thrift; the parishes of the north tend to be large because their populations have been small. But look south. The landscape, like a portly yeoman, breathes a more privileged air. The fields are much bigger, the farm buildings grander. There have been the surpluses and the time, over the centuries, to introduce all manner of grace notes and to impose an artful design not only on the show-piece parkland of Penrice but on the landscape as a whole: note, for instance, how the judiciously planted pines around the bijou little church of Nicholaston – virtually rebuilt in the 1890s by Olive Talbot (1842–1894) of Penrice, as a memorial to her father, C. R. M. Talbot – are answered, delightfully, by those gathered round a driveway a short distance down the road. Further along the road, and past the fake 'ruins' (dating

back to the 1790s) at the Oxwich turn-off, there comes into view one of the most appealing buildings in Gower, the Home Farm granary, raised from the ground on stone 'mushrooms' – to keep vermin at bay – and topped with an idiosyncratic lantern and weathervane. It's a landscape mellowed over recent centuries by custom and indulgence; but the symbol of its original, brute power, the massive Norman stronghold of Penrice Castle, is still visible among the parkland's trees.

With a string of such castles, the Normans held Gower's richest farmland – very much as they did in south Pembrokeshire – and Cefn Bryn came to represent a dividing line between a relatively prosperous English-speaking south and a relatively indigent Welsh-speaking north and north-east. The cultural schism, obvious from a glance at the place names on a map, is less pronounced than it used to be; but until the later 19th century, when communication by road was still difficult, the Bryn could be a significant social barrier. Many Gower men, unable to find farming or quarrying jobs, became mariners – and only then, in some cases, might they have had the opportunity of encountering compatriots from the 'other side', as Horatio Tucker relates in his *Gower Gleanings*: 'Many south Gower men were more at home in Santos, or Iquiqui [Iquique], than in *Langenny* [Llangennith] or *Rinnason* [Reynoldston]; in fact, some of them had never set foot on the north side of Cefn Bryn, but were acquainted with North Gower men through having met them abroad.'

Descending from our reservoir observation post and our contemplation of ineffable immensities of space and time, David and I are welcomed back to self-important reality by an official notice on the small, windowless shed at the bottom of the steps informing us that it's a 'Category B confined space'.

Not surprisingly, Cefn Bryn forms part of the 56-km Gower Way, a walking route established by those indispensable guardians and celebrators of Gower, the Gower Society, to inaugurate the millennium. It links communities and points of interest across the ancient lordship of Gower, from Penlle'r Castell on Mynydd y Gwair in the north-east to the old coastguard lookout building opposite Worms Head in the south-west.[5] The fifty marker stones distributed at roughly 1-km intervals along the route – there are two between the reservoir and the ridgeway's junction with the Cilibion–Reynoldston road – are Pennant

---

[5] A pack containing three informative sectional maps of the Gower Way is available at tourist information centres or from the society.

sandstone blocks from Cwmrhydyceirw Quarry in Morriston; they served originally as coping stones for the Townhill Service Reservoir (early 1900s), before Welsh Water donated them to the Gower Society as way markers. Each is carved with its own number, 'The Gower Way' and the society's name in both languages,[6] and the society's portcullis emblem, representing its motto, 'Protecting Gower for all its worth'. Without the diligent guardianship of the Gower Society, the whole area of the old lordship, Swansea included, would today be immensely poorer in heritage and environmental terms. Established initially by a handful of enthusiasts who called themselves the Gowermen, it was inaugurated formally as the Gower Society in 1948. They were plunged immediately into battle, defending Rhosili Bay from plans to build a Butlin's-style holiday camp there.[7] Their successful resistance established them as the biggest local amenity society in Wales, and they've gone on since then to win (and sometimes lose) many campaigns on Gower's behalf, from high-profile triumphs such as saving Swansea Castle from demolition,[8] to more low-key and toilsome endeavours, such as opposing the piecemeal suburbanisation of the peninsula.

On our gradual descent from the ridge, as we head towards Arthur's Stone, we pass an orientation table placed in 1977 by the local chapter of Rotary International. Its plinth is made of the same coarse quartz-conglomerates as the ridge itself. It used to be assumed that the 35-tonne Arthur's Stone was a similarly local chunk of Devonian conglomerates, but it turns out to be an erratic, carried here by glaciers of the ice age from an outcrop of Millstone Grit on the northern edge of the coalfield some 50 km away.

Visible on its false crest from much of north Gower, this 4000- to 5000-year-old megalithic tomb has excited numerous legends and much speculation. Friends from Reynoldston who brought me here as a child used to claim that it was the final resting place of King Arthur: we'd crawl beneath the massive capstone, fearful that it might slip from its four stubby supports and crush us, and we'd swear we could hear the great king's blood coursing around the boulders on which we were spreadeagled. Later we'd hear versions of the popular tale that the stone, an irritant to Arthur's foot as he bestrode the northern shore of the Burry Inlet, had been shaken from his boot and tossed over the estuary – to land on Cefn Bryn.

[6] Interestingly, 'society' becomes, in Welsh, not the anticipated 'cymdeithas' but 'cyfeillion', meaning 'friends'.
[7] The biggest structure to have been imposed on this stretch of coast was, thankfully, a 'virtual' one: a futuristic hospital which the BBC's special effects department mocked up for a 2007 episode of *Dr Who*.
[8] In 1957, wanting to clear the site for post-war development, Swansea councillors declared the castle variously 'a shambles' and 'a shocking thing'.

GORSE

River yearning seaward, the sea's
influx pressing upstream, slowing the race

and slowed in turn, as shouldering waves
roll free beneath cool river fingers . . .

I fill again,
      as the river fills,
            with skies of the milky fire
that crackles on the bank. And the air
I breathe – of coconut, of peach – fills me
with you,
            with she
            who has long since
            deepened with silence.

Wash and backwash, the river
swollen, sea-deep with gorse-light,
      (my tongue breaking
      to the peach of your mouth . . .)

honeyed air of gorse,
                        and dark scent
in my beard – come and gone –
a musk of you, your coaxed most inward
      scent of woman.

Wash and backwash,
brinks of sand
                  plashing on the flow,
eddies whispering in the river's ears
a froth of grasses, of butterfly wings

till tide and current

lie belly on belly, spilling their banks,
all need converging
                        in the one water.

Its Welsh name, Maen Ceti (Ceti's stone), occurs first in a triad published in the 16th century, the raising of the cromlech's capstone being described as 'one of the three mighty achievements of the Isle of Britain'. But it may not have been 'raised' in that sense. Archaeologists tend to think the tomb was constructed by digging under the capstone and inserting the nine uprights beneath it. Then the whole structure would probably have been covered by a vast mound of rubble and earth – as suggested by the smaller stones scattered in a rough circle around the cromlech. When and how a great slice of the capstone became detached from the main body – to lie alongside it, rendering five of the uprights redundant – remains a mystery.

To walk Cefn Bryn from stream to stream, as it were, you'd need to carry on, via Hill End, to Burry Pill at Stembridge. But on this occasion, with liquid of another sort in mind, we decide to stick with the King Arthur theme. We wend our way through the bracken to the pub of that name in Reynoldston, for a pint of Tomos Watkin OSB. Brewed in Swansea, and one of the most flavoursome bitters in Wales, OSB is a fitting libation, on the threshold of Cefn Bryn, for toasting the tutelars, ancient and modern, of this green and numinous backbone of Gower.

****

LIMESTONE

The defining genius of peninsular Gower is that great geological contrarian, limestone – boaster, on the one hand, of vast, involuted cliffscapes, theatrically responsive to every changing mood of light, and hoarder, on the other, of the darkest of subterranean secrets. Limestone comprises two thirds of the peninsula.

Above sea level, the land of Gower asserts itself, as we have seen, at two distinctive altitudes. The older, higher ground – of Cefn Bryn, Rhosili Down (the highest point), Llanmadog Hill – is Devonian Red Sandstone, reaching in general a height of about 185 m. If the red sandstone summits of Gower look down on the younger strata of the Carboniferous Limestone, it is nevertheless the limestone peneplain – a wave-cut and sea-indented plateau 70 m high, stretching 24 km from Mumbles to Rhosili – that commands the greater attention. The magnificent headlands of Pwlldu, Oxwich, Port Eynon and Rhosili that rear out into the Severn Sea were, like the rest of Gower's blocky limestone, laid down some 350 million years ago in warm, subtropical waters – the sea then being 70 m higher, relative to the land, than it is today.

As good a beach as any on which to contemplate limestone is Pwlldu, almost the only place on Gower's southern coast to retain a Welsh name: it means 'black pool', after the dark gathering of stream water that is dammed behind the great storm bank of sea-rolled shingle – which makes percussive, chatty music as you trudge along it. Indeed, the limestone here is a treat to all the senses. Take a pebble, note the minuscule flecks and veins of pink, yellow, blue, green on its silvery-grey surface; smell the sun on it and the sea; taste the salt on it; put the pebble – a small one – in your mouth, roll it around in the risen fullness of saliva, clink it against the warm, living calcite of your teeth, and consider the deaths of millions of sea creatures millions of years ago that went into the making of this simple stone and of the rocks that surround you.

That limestone is composed of the calcareous remains of an immense variety of once living things – shells, bones, corals – makes it the most memorious of rocks. This skeletal debris is accreted layer by compressed layer on the sea floor, in conditions similar to those that prevail today in limestone-forming areas such as the Pacific, the Bahamas and the Persian Gulf. Fossilised remains of marine animals can be seen in the limestone of bays such as Three Cliffs and Bracelet; and at the disused Clement's Quarry in Oystermouth, now a car park, there is an imposing face of blackish limestone, particularly rich in fossils, which yielded a fossil shell that is named after the village (*Spirifer oystermouthensis*). Because the limestone here, unlike that of the headlands, has not been uplifted, you are able to experience the *frisson* of walking on a seabed that is 300 million years old. While the bedding planes of Clement's Quarry have retained their ancient, horizontal axis, those of the headlands – Great Tor being among the most striking examples – demonstrate a dramatic uplifting of almost 90 degrees, as a result of colossal convulsions of the earth's crust about 280 million years ago, which buckled the strata into the upfolds (anticlines) and downfolds (synclines) that are so characteristic of limestone country. Such was the violence of the buckling that the strata suffered major dislocations along powerful fault lines, allowing the sea to cut deeply inland, as at Caswell, Pwlldu, Three Cliffs, Oxwich, Mewslade and Broughton.

The faulting of limestone and its solubility in water leads to both erosion and transformational re-creation. Rainwater will slowly dissolve an outcrop along its bedding planes and joint systems, creating characteristic fissures – along which river water will carve a passage into the strata, ultimately creating virtually dry riverbeds (as in the upper reaches of Bishopston Valley), underground channels and caves. Gower is honeycombed with caves, many of which, surely, have yet to be discovered. One of the most spectacular – and dangerous – is Llethryd Swallet in the Green Cwm, with its Great Hall and its astoundingly beautiful calcite curtains, stalagmites and stalactites, which have to drip for all of a thousand years before adding a mere inch to their length.

Above ground too, water's patient enlargements of the limestone's flaws have left distinctive traces. Broad Pool, for instance, besides the Cilibion to Reynoldston road, where I remember dozens of people skating in a harsh 1960s winter, is probably a sinkhole – through which, normally, water would disappear – which has become clogged by clay deposited during the most recent ice age, thus keeping water at the surface. And a stone's throw in the direction of Reynoldston, there begins a stretch of road which in childhood we knew as 'the switchbacks' – a series of humps and troughs over which, if your driver could be goaded into driving fast enough, you'd feel your pelvic floor do an orgasmic turn as the car itself, at every humpback, momentarily took to the skies. These undulations, considerably diminished since those days, result from the collapse of underground caverns created by the dissolving action of water on limestone.

Limestone's genesis in living organisms, its erosive habits and clandestine creations appeal to something in us that few other rocks succeed in touching. 'If it form the one landscape that we, the inconstant ones, / Are consistently homesick for,' wrote W.H. Auden in 'In Praise of Limestone' (1951), 'this is chiefly / because it dissolves in water . . .' He was much moved by the fact that, like people, the forms that limestone assumes over time are determined as much by its faults as by its substance: '. . . when I try to imagine a faultless love / Or the life to come, what I hear is the murmur / Of underground streams, what I see is a limestone landscape.'

Pwlldu in its heyday was one of Gower's busiest quarries, or 'flotquars' as they were called locally. Quarrying is believed to have started here in the late 17th century and continued until 1889, employing at its peak, in the early 19th century, some 200 men and women from the nearby villages of Bishopston, Kittle, Pennard and Parkmill. The workers' formidable thirsts were catered for by no fewer than five pubs – the Bull, the New Inn, the Star, the Beaufort and the Ship, the last two of which became the private houses that exist today; Beaufort House still bears the pub's name panel on its eastern-facing wall. An obvious reminder of the vast tonnages of limestone that were shipped from Pwlldu – chiefly to Devon and Cornwall – are the parallel trenches that scar the headland like a giant's plough marks, down which the quarried stones were sledded, or rolled and barred. The 'needles' and the 'ring rocks' down on the beach are no doubt the remains of a quay wall, but the stone itself seems not to have been loaded at such a quayside. Although the quarrying and the stockpiling of stones on the shore was pursued all year round, it was only during the summer months that the limestone was shipped out of Pwlldu – in skiffs known as limestone tars with a crew of three or four, which would bring various goods over for Gower people, including jumpers knitted during the winter by West Country hands. At the industry's peak, there would be up to thirty boats in the bay at one time. Each would pull alongside a pile of stones and, before the tide retreated, the crew would scuttle the vessel by opening the sea-cocks; as the skiff rested on the bottom, they would close the cocks, so that the hull remained full of water when the tide went out, thus providing the means of breaking the impact of the first blocks as they were hefted aboard. When the boat was fully laden, they would open the sea-cocks to drain the vessel, close the cocks again and make ready to sail on the incoming tide. Another major memento of industrial days is Pwlldu's radiant bank of limestone cobbles, which seems the very essence of the place. It may constitute the dam that brought about Pwlldu's name, but it is far from being some primordial accumulation, having been formed in the last 300 years from detritus left over from the quarrymen's blasting on the headland.

There are less manifest souvenirs. Few, probably, of those aboard the thirty or forty sumptuous yachts that drop anchor now and then for champers at Pwlldu can be aware that a metre or two beneath their fibreglass bottoms lies a ship-shaped pile of stones, retaining still the outline of a limestone tar that never made it back to Dumnonia.

sweeping the cliffside's

exuberant gorse,

a kestrel's shade.

****

THE BALLAD OF PWLLDU HEAD

One long gone winter's time ago
    The press to Swansea came
To grab for war Welsh sailing boys
    In the king of England's name.

They say that more than ninety souls
    Were snatched from home and street
And, crammed below the *Caesar*'s deck,
    Were despatched to join the fleet.

'You're off,' said Lieutenant Gaborian,
    'To lawless foreign lands.
The Parly-vous wants drivin' out
    And the king, God bless 'im, wants hands.'

The *Caesar* sailed and her restive freight
    So loth to leave Swansea town,
Were tied hands high to the timbers
    And all hatches were battened down.

The ship, they feared, was a poor match
    For the tricksy Severn Sea,
And they met the swell at Mumbles Head
    With a chill of anxiety.

By Oxwich Point both wind and tide
    Were standing in her way,
So the captain turned her back to seek
    The calm of Swansea Bay.

Mumbles Head he was looking for,
    But the rocks of Pwlldu he found:
As darkness fell and the breakers crashed
    The *Caesar* ran aground.

'Save yourselves!' Gaborian roared
    To the men dismayed on deck.
Those bound below they left behind
    To perish with the wreck.

The *Caesar*, holed and boulder-wedged,
    Began to take in water,
And slow, as slow the tide rose up,
    Began the captives' slaughter.

They screamed, they stamped and pleas did shout
    Their souls, sweet God, to save . . .
But all, by dawn's departed tide,
    Was silent as the grave.

And when they held a court martial
    Gaborian was acclaimed
As he whose skills had saved the crew;
    For the ship's loss fog was blamed.

Of those who died in the *Caesar*'s hold
    Not a word in court was said.
And Pwlldu too, the summers through,
    Keeps dark about its dead.

But in winter on that naked point
    You'll find a crowd of stones
Telling of wreckage beneath the turf,
    A shipful of tyrannized bones.

PAVILAND

Gower's welcoming, domesticated landscapes can give way dramatically at the farmland's fringes to severely unaccommodating vistas. One of the peninsula's most dramatic and sometimes forbidding stretches of coastline, between Port Eynon Point and Mewslade, is, paradoxically, the site of Gower's earliest known human habitation. Millennia of relentless marine violence have churned the limestone foreshore into a jagged moonscape of swirl-holes, grykes and knife-edged troughs, almost impossible to find a path through and ruinous of any ship cast haplessly among them. Yet here, some 29,900 years ago, in a cave at Paviland known as Goat's Hole, there lived, and died, what many have considered to be the first Welshman – a rather anachronistic claim, admittedly, and one undermined, furthermore, by the later discovery of human teeth, dated to *c.*250,000 BC, in Pontnewydd cave in Denbighshire. And he and his kind were by no means the first hominids to visit Goat's Hole: the cave has also yielded a flint implement left there over 70,000 years ago by Neanderthal man.

Goat's Hole, which is about 5 m wide and 20 m deep, is best approached at low water, by way of a deep, rubbled gully leading down from the clifftop bordering Paviland Manor farm; a dangerous alternative route, along a narrow sheep-path halfway up the western side of the gully, which has sometimes tempted those frustrated by the tide, has led several to their deaths. From a sandy spit at the gully's seaward end, a turn to the right and an easy scramble up a steep shoulder of rock will lead you to the mouth of the cave.

The cave was first investigated in 1822 by two amateur archaeologists, the industrialist and botanist Lewis Weston Dillwyn of Penllergaer and Mary Theresa Talbot of Penrice Castle, who had heard that people living nearby had made some interesting discoveries at Goat's Hole. Their finds excited the interest of the Reverend William Buckland, already renowned as Oxford's first professor of geology. It was during Buckland's subsequent exploration in 1823 that the skeleton – headless, and only the left half of it – was discovered. It was, at the time,

by far the earliest human bone find in Britain, and the first instance of the scientific recovery of fossil human remains in the world – although Buckland was entirely unaware of the historic significance of his discovery. Investigating numerous caves in Britain and mainland Europe, he was on a somewhat quixotic mission to prove that there had been no human life in these islands before Noah's flood. His discovery in the cave floor of human bones along with the remains of long-extinct animals such as the mammoth and the woolly rhinoceros could have fatally undermined his theory, but he made up his mind that the human bones were of considerably more recent provenance than those of the animals. That they had been stained with red ochre and were associated with perforated sea shells, ivory wands and bracelets suggested to him, eventually, that they were the bones of a woman – and he had a neat explanation up his Regency sleeve as to the when and why of her residence here. 'The circumstances of the remains of a British camp existing on the hill immediately above this cave,' he opined in his *Reliquiae Deluvianae*, 'seems to throw much light on the character and date of the woman under consideration – and whatever may have been her occupation, the vicinity of a camp would afford a motive for residence, as well as a means of subsistence, in what is now so exposed and uninviting a solitude . . .' Thus was born the legend of the Red Lady of Paviland. But the torridly imaginative cleric was wrong on at least two counts. Not only did the bones turn out to be those of a young man, but radiocarbon dating in the 20th century revealed them to be far more than a couple of thousand years old. The bones have been difficult to date, because they were treated with preservatives soon after their discovery. An early scientific dating put them at 18,000 years old; this was later adjusted to 26,000 years. But in 2007 new dating techniques established that the bones – which were probably of African ancestry – were 29,900 years old, confirming Paviland as the most important archaeological site in these islands of the Early Upper Palaeolithic period. Indeed, it has been suggested that the name usually given to the earliest modern humans in Europe, 'Cro-Magnons', after a discovery in France in 1868, should be replaced by 'Pavilandians'.

Significant traces of the 'British camp' to which Buckland refers – one of Gower's nine Iron Age promontory forts – survive on the formidable cliff of Yellow Top, over 60 m above the cave, in the banks and ditches that defended the Celtic settlement on the landward side.

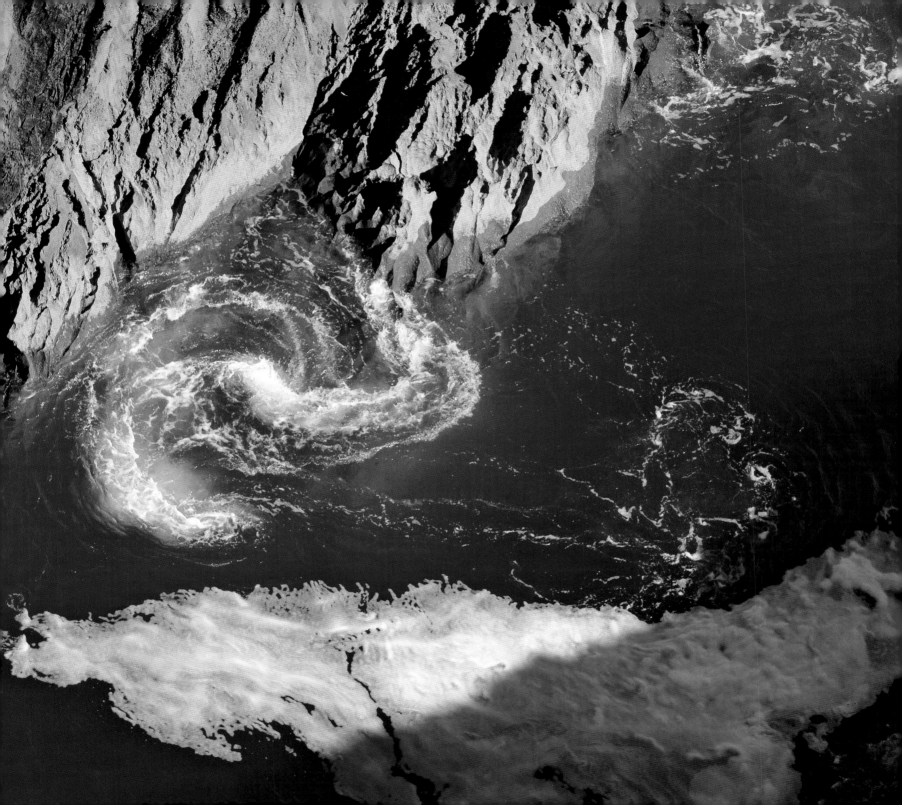

GOAT'S HOLE, PAVILAND

When bronze lay dreaming, and the ice
hoarded oceans to the far north,
this huge vulva, aloof in the rock
to sea's thrust or man's, was home
to the hunter, his forge and grave.

Long wise to death, they
offered him outward with skull
of mammoth, lyric shells – charms
that so beguiled his finders
they thought they'd unearthed a woman.

In words of flint, in the dark
language of his own ruddled bones
the silt whispers news of his world:

a phrase of worked ivory outlines
an arm; your thumb's fit
with a dimpled stone sounds the voice
of trails, great voice of the herds
that were tidal here an age before
seas had discovered their plain.
Charred bones light a fire, speak
warm in-comings from mammoth-steppe cold –

to leap of shadow, meat-smoke
and the endless skill of fingers.

We piece back the pieces.

Though more than we have held
is hidden here, we, who have trailed
among the stars, are pleased to remember
what the earth has forgotten: furs
and baskets and tools of wood, the skull
of the man, his intelligence:

it's this softer thing – finer
than a flint's edge, tougher than stone –
that fashions amazement, keeps us guessing.

**these sheep-shorn ramparts,
two thousand years on, still force
a change of tack**

If Goat's Hole seems inhospitable to us today, it can scarcely have seemed less so to Paviland man and his fellow hunter-gatherers, although the recent re-dating of the remains suggests that they lived in warmer conditions than the tundral cold of previous assumptions. Nevertheless, they were clinging to existence at the edge of the habitable world. In what scientists categorise as a 'continental and cold' climate, their summers would have been relatively warm but their winters freezing. To the north, in Snowdonia, there would probably have been glaciers, and so much water was retained by the burgeoning ice fields further north that much of what would become the Severn Sea was a steppe-like plane, grazed by the herds whose wanderings these hunters were yoked to. With sea levels some 80 m lower than those of today, they would have been situated about 100 km inland. The view from the mouth of their cave, millennia before Britain became an island, would have been of grassy flatlands extending towards an horizon dominated by the Exmoor hills.

'The Red Lady' may not have been 'the first Welshman', but there can be no dispute that his ritual interment in Goat's Hole cave makes this the earliest known site of religious observance in Wales – not that the religious beliefs of those who performed the obsequies can be more than guessed at. Some of the artefacts and remains dug up at Paviland are on display in Swansea Museum, but the Red Lady himself resides far from home – in the Pitt Rivers Museum, Oxford. On my first visit in the 1970s, the 'dark brick-red colour' of his bones drew me straight to his resting place beneath the louring dinosaurs and soaring arches of that magnificent Victorian essay in iron, stone and glass. Composing myself reverentially before the Red Lady's cabinet, I felt a tap on my arm. 'These, sir,' said a caretaker, 'are not the real bones. They are casts. If you'd like to see the real ones, please follow me.' He led me down into the basement, pulled open a drawer – and there they were, the actual bones of the Red Lady of Paviland. I asked in vain – with the similarly purloined 'Elgin marbles' in mind – if Wales could have the skeleton back. In 2008, when the (real) Red Lady came 'home' for a brief residency at the National Museum in Cardiff, it was a question that many were still asking.

****

INLAND

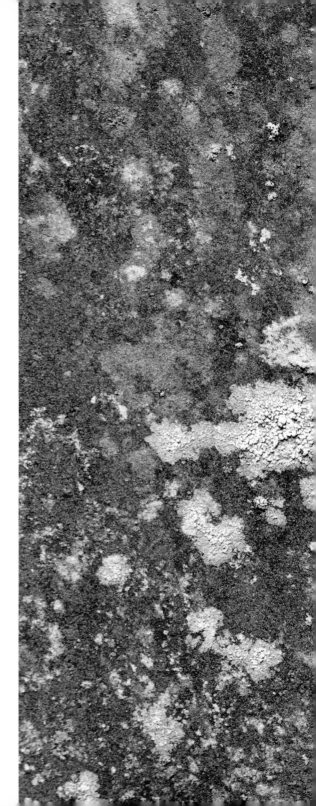

THE CASTLES OF THE CLEANSING

Ethnic cleansing. This ugly expression is not a term that most people would associate with what for centuries has been a backwater, mercifully unattended by 'interesting times'. Britain's first Area of Outstanding Natural Beauty, the websites boast, with its golden beaches, sun-dappled moors and . . . romantic castles. Why so many castles in so small an area? To attempt an answer is to peer into an oubliette of land-grabbing violence and misery all too reminiscent of scenes from our own times in Rwanda, Bosnia, Darfur.

There are many more castles in Gower than meet the casual eye, although they make nothing like the ostentatious statements of power and prestige – and ultimately, in many cases, of culture – fanfared by castles such as Oystermouth and Penrice. These older, less declamatory fortifications tend to elide with the landscape's contours, their outlines fogged by time and blurred, often, by gorse, bracken or woodland.

If the Bronze Age, with its economic surpluses and cosmological strivings, was a relatively peaceable era, the same cannot be claimed for the age of iron – the metal (still essential to modern society) that overwhelmed the Bronze Age world and established Celtic civilisation as the progenitive culture of the land that would eventually cohere as Cymru (Wales). The twenty or so Iron Age hill forts and promontory forts discernible in Gower today, most densely concentrated in the west, were constructed not to safeguard the population against any external threat but to defend local tribes against each others' predatory inclinations. Some were no more sophisticated than a palisaded bank-and-ditch isolating the seaward tip of a promontory, such as that on Horse Cliff. Others, chief among them Cilifor, near Llanrhidian, and the Bulwark (or Llanmadoc hill fort), were extensive, complex structures – 2.9 ha and .9 ha respectively – that would have served a variety of purposes: a fold for animals, a focal point for sacrament and ritual, a centre for seasonal agricultural activities, a refuge at times of conflict, and the local chieftain's stronghold. From a distance, and in certain lights, some of these diminished structures seem almost

indistinguishable from their hill- and clifftop sites; but given shadow-casting sunlight, there's no mistaking the three concentric ramparts of Cilifor, for instance, or the banks and ditches of the Hardings Down fortresses or those of the Bulwark; and at close quarters, 2000 years after the time of their construction, they are still formidable barriers. If the Iron Age fortifications appear to be relatively subdued presences in today's landscape, in contrast with the showpiece castles of the Normans, the largest of them would have stood originally as boastful beacons of a tribe's manpower, wealth and aggressive potential, with their forbidding *murus gallicus* consisting of a boxlike grid of timbers filled with rubble, faced with laid masonry and topped with a spiky palisade; a fort's lime-washed defences would ensure that it was visible for miles.

Hill forts such as the Bulwark, Cilifor and Pen-y-gaer (overlooking what is now Penclawdd) must have been a troubling sight for the Roman conquistadors sailing up the Burry Inlet, through enemy territory, to their strategically important garrison at Leucarum (Llwchwr) only a few miles away. Was there a bloody showdown, therefore, with the Celts of Gower, or was some kind of accommodation reached, with the Romans agreeing a 'hands off' policy in exchange for non-interference in their imperial affairs? Little is known of the Iron Age inhabitants of Gower – not even, it seems, whether they were members of the Silures, the tribe of south-east Wales which provided the most implacable opposition to Roman occupation of all the British tribes, or whether they belonged to the Demetae, the tribe of south-west Wales. The long-standing assumption that the Demetae were relatively accepting of Roman occupation has been called into question by the discovery, in 2003, of two Roman forts at Dinefwr, Llandeilo, just as recent Roman finds in Gower have led to revision of the traditional belief that the Romans pushed no further into the peninsula than Oystermouth.

Whatever the Roman presence in Gower, there has been little evidence unearthed so far to suggest much disruption to indigenous agricultural ways. In the vacuum left by Roman withdrawal from Britain in the early 5th century, Irish expansionism – which would leave indelible traces in Pembrokeshire, Carmarthenshire and Breconshire – seems on the whole to have passed Gower by. As for the Vikings (or Northmen), whose harrying of the Welsh coast was first recorded in the mid 9th century, there are few indications of any enduring settlement in the peninsula, in spite of Gower having more Norse finds than any other part of Wales (they number five). Swansea is fondly attached to the notion that it was founded by some Viking magnate called Sweyn (or Sveinn) who established a base on an 'ey' (island) in the mouth of the Tawe, hence 'Sweyn's ey'. The iconography of the Guildhall (1934) makes much of the city's supposed Scandinavian origins, with Viking prows jutting out of the clock faces on its tower, masks of Sweyn and his adventurers adorning certain keystones, and bronze handrails with Viking ship motifs. But Swansea's Viking provenance, most historians agree, is largely a myth, supported only by that 'z'-sounding second 's' in the word Swansea, which may embody some memory of the possessor of that long-gone, river-mouth 'ey'. Some other local place names, such as Worms Head and Burry Holms, may possibly have Scandinavian origins, and there's no denying a brief history of Viking pillage hereabouts, notably the destruction by Danes of St Cenydd's *clas* (Celtic monastery) at Llangennith in 986. If such raids had relatively few long-term consequences, the same cannot be said of the invasion by those descendants of the Northmen who had settled in the lower Seine valley, the Normans.

What the Vikings began, the Normans carried through to devastating effect, annihilating in less than a decade a way of life that had evolved, with few major disjunctions, over thousands of years. The castles that display themselves so prominently throughout the peninsula were not in the vanguard of Norman military might; rather, they are triumphant declarations that the conquerors' mission has been accomplished, the natives have been removed, and may the settlers' enrichment proceed. The essential, lethal groundwork was effected by much simpler castles of compacted earth and wood, at least three of which – folded unassumingly into the landscape – may be seen today: Barland (north-east of Barland Common, Bishopston), Penmaen, and Penrice Old Castle (also known as Mounty Bank), a huge, overgrown mound just outside Penrice village.

The Normans conquered England, as everyone knows, in 1066. But it took them and the Anglo-Normans over two more centuries to bring a stubbornly irrepressible Wales under their overall control. The incursion started in a piecemeal way, with earldoms established along the Wales–England border, and seizures by conquest of Gwynedd,

four feet whiten
the miles of shore;
two shadows join hands

Whit Monday washout,
red spade abandoned
in the deluged castle

south-west Wales and Glamorgan: these areas constituted the burgeoning March, a group of independent lordships ruled by Anglo-Norman lords. The commote of Gŵyr (Gower), part of the kingdom of Ystrad Tywi, was among the last regions of southern Wales to yield to Norman rule. By 1095, Gower had suffered numerous Norman raids; then, in about 1106 Henry I, blatantly contemptuous of the Welsh rulers, 'gave' Gower to his friend Henry de Beaumont, the first earl of Warwick, who, in order to take possession of a gift that was doubtless reluctant to be given, began a purposeful assault. The politics of Henry de Beaumont's territorial theft are relatively clear, but how in practical, bloody terms he began that appropriation is largely guesswork.

Not surprisingly, there's a distinct cluster of Norman strongholds around Oxwich Bay – for Oxwich, like Swansea Bay, is an obvious and vulnerable point of ingress for any invader, with its shallow, calm waters, and over 3 km of open, sandy beach.

Here, as at Swansea, the keels of Norman ships – from bases on the English side of the Severn Sea – would have scrunched ashore, and awestruck local farmers would surely have watched in horror as hundreds of helmeted and chain-mailed soldiers spilled onto the sands, many of them mounted on warhorses mightier than any creature that had ever shaken the shores of Gower. Or perhaps the campaign was a combination of both sea and land attack, from the lordships which the colonialists were consolidating either side of Ystrad Tywi. But a campaign of the mailed fist there must surely have been: polite entreaties advertising greener grass on the north side of Cefn Bryn would hardly have persuaded the populace of southern Gower obligingly to remove itself.

The small population of Gower, living in scattered farmsteads and hamlets, was no match for the Normans' specialised, professional military machine, nor was any Welsh military opposition. The two peoples had different military traditions. The Welsh, with their loosely organised, part-time infantry outfits, were adept mountain and guerrilla warriors, using military force mainly to pursue feuds and to seize booty. They lacked the technology and organisation of the Normans, who had perfected the deployment of heavy cavalry on the plains of northern France, enabling them to seize and hold the arable land which produced a society's wealth – experience which was decisive in their seizure of Wales's low-lying coastal farmland.

Exploiting both surprise and Welsh political disunity, the Normans probably encountered little organised opposition at first as they stormed inland, visiting on the people the 'shock and awe' of their ferociously efficient sword-work, and setting fire to every native hut and farmstead. Those lucky enough to escape the slaughter must have headed desperately through the smoke for the slopes of Cefn Bryn in the hope of finding some respite and shelter on the other side of the hill.

With the natives reeling from the assault, and before retaliatory forces could be mustered, the Normans would have devoted all their resources to building castles – initially, as noted earlier, simple but sturdy structures built of earth, rubble and wood. Their reliance on castles to consolidate their conquests was the key to their success, and it would change the way warfare was conducted in Wales. At Swansea, on a site just north of the present castle, they established the motte-and-bailey castle that would serve as hub for the 'pacification' of their lordship of Gower. Similar structures, or simpler ringwork castles, were thrown up further down the coast, at places such as Oystermouth, Pennard, Penmaen and Penrice. The much larger stone castles that were later erected on many of these sites generally obliterated all traces of the earthwork castles. But some were not rebuilt in stone, one of the most complete and accessible survivors being Penmaen Old Castle, perched on the easternmost tip of Penmaen Burrows in a commanding position overlooking Three Cliffs Bay. Some of the treasures of this enigmatic headland – legendary site of the 'lost village' of Stedworlango – are difficult to find in the summer, thanks to the bracken and coarse grasses: a Neolithic burial chamber, the remains of a medieval church, the 'pillow mounds' where the Normans raised their rabbits. But the old castle stands proud of the vegetation, winter and summer, its deep, rock-cut ditch and massive, circular embankment of limestone rubble presenting still, after 900 years, a daunting obstacle. The embankment would have been topped with a timber palisade, and there was a large timber gate-tower on the north-east side of the fort, with a wooden bridge over the ditch.

Having established such footholds along the coast, and assigned manorial plots to his kinsmen and retainers, Henry de Beaumont would have wasted no time in shipping in peasants from England to repopulate the 'cleansed' farmland. To quote the historian John

Davies, 'as the history of Ireland amply proves, a dense settlement of peasants is always a more effective way of consolidating conquest than a thin layer of gentry'.

It may have taken a further century for the occupation to spread to north-west Gower. Weobley Castle – a fortified manor house (in its later manifestation), rather than a true castle – was the conquerors' domineering presence on the north Gower coast. The clearance of the indigenous population from the Llangennith–Llanmadoc–Llanrhidian tract may not have been as brutal a clean sweep as was the southern evacuation, for various Celtic place names and customs survived the general expulsion; some traditions, such as the Llanmadoc *Mabsant*, a festival celebrating the parish's patron saint, Madoc, were still being observed in the early 20th century.

Although the Normans' enforced lordship of Gower embraced the old commote of Gŵyr in its entirety, they took little interest in the relatively barren, hilly terrain east of Llanrhidian, which extended northwards to the Black Mountains; they exercised only a vague suzerainty over territory which was incapable of sustaining intensive agriculture. The natives were welcome to their Welshry, or Gower *Wallicana* as the north-eastern reaches came to be called.

The indigenous Welsh did not take their dispossession lying down. In 1960, archaeological excavations at Penmaen showed that a Welsh attack had reduced the massive timbers of the gate-tower to charred stumps, and the soil of the adjacent rampart had been reddened by fire. Between 1113 and 1217, the Welsh resistance made at least half a dozen devastating raids into the Englishry, but as soon as they destroyed the earth and timber castles the Normans would build them back up again. By 1300, the chief castles had been rebuilt in stone, their defensive role augmented by the heavily fortified towers of some dozen stone churches, chief among them Oystermouth, Ilston, Penrice, Oxwich, Cheriton and Llanrhidian, which were crucial points of refuge during Welsh raids into the peninsula (the Normans had scorned the Welsh for their lack of stone churches).

Even after the killing of Llywelyn ap Gruffudd, the 'last' Prince of Wales,[1] in 1282, the Anglo-Normans could not afford to relax their guard, for there were still sporadic challenges to alien rule, and, during the Revolt of Owain Glyndŵr (1400–1415), there was a decidedly methodical challenge, which saw native forces once again – but for the last time – overrunning Gower.

[1] That title perhaps belongs more properly to Owain Glyndŵr (c.1354–1415/6)

Work on the stone castles began around the mid 13th century in most cases, after the lordship of Gower had come into the possession of the brutal de Breos dynasty. As powerfully defensive structures, most of the castles certainly saw violent action, but they were designed also to overawe the natives and to impress the Anglo-Norman neighbours – as size and complexity gradually gave way, in more peaceable times, to fine embellishment. This development is illustrated by the four castles associated with the Penrice dynasty. The first of them, Old Penrice Castle (or the Mounty Bank), served Henry de Beaumont's purposes well in the early, desperately unsettled stages of the occupation. It was probably built by the de Penres family from Devon, who later abandoned the ringwork for the stone-built Penrice Castle, the largest of all the Gower castles. The family, becoming Mansels in the early 15th century, eventually decamped to Oxwich Castle, which they rebuilt, in the early 16th century, as a vast and palatial mansion house, its castle-like features performing now a decorative rather than a defensive role. After an interlude at Margam Abbey, they finally 'upgraded' to the neo-classical, 'new' Penrice Castle in the 1770s. Here, after several more changes of name, they still live – although the family's formerly extensive Penrice holdings, plundered from the natives by their Mounty Bank forebears all those centuries ago, are now much diminished.

Swansea Castle was the lordship's *caput*, but Oystermouth was generally the favourite residence of the lords of Gower. The most ornate of the Gower castles, with its capacious living accommodation and beautifully fenestrated chapel block, Oystermouth has been described by John Davies, in a recent book of a hundred things to see in Wales before you die, as '*yr hyfrytaf o holl gestyll Cymru*' (the most delightful of all the castles of Wales).

If the castles of our conquerors have by now conquered even our affections – as harmlessly they may, in a freshly enlivened, post-devolution (and perhaps, soon, postcolonial) Wales – it's as well to remember their original purpose and its application to a realm much larger than peninsular Gower. In 500 castles of the earlier, earthwork kind throughout Wales and the borderlands, the British Empire could be said to have laid its foundations.

tide in, skiers out
– the dollar signs carved
from shore to shore

****

PARC

Here he set his English elms
and his cattle and his deer,

and hereby over all,
with stones hewn by his cousin the Norman
    did he raise in artful wildness
    the ruin of a tower,
from close under heaven enjoying command
of all lands sound, sweet and fertile
     'twixt the bounteous sea

and those sour, safely distant, Welsh-speaking hills.

The new man, cruising the sward in his Rolls,
    farms it through the bank.
Brambles root mid-field, the fencing sags
as he waits on a deal or permission to build.
You can hear through the crows the throats
he sits on, see in flung gateways the mouths
    his farming fails to feed.

I watched through one summer
his elm trees die. No May will plump
this copse with shade, an ending is here,
    it is time to re-plant.
But this man will not, nor any of his kind.

Something beyond him is taking its course.

SEASIDE – A HAIKU CALENDAR

from the ice-rubbled
foreshore, twenty pale chunks
detach themselves and fly

sand blown through
tinselly twigs – the first washed-up
Christmas tree of spring

gull hooked, trailing
from its beak a yard of line –
o for a gun

Whit Monday high tide –
the jellyfish that happens
to be a balloon

through the haze
across the bay – new-mown,
a field in the sky

smacking lushly ashore
from the bay long becalmed –
the vanished ferry's wake

the seal's head and mine
bobbing face to face
on the tide

tide's in, barbie's done
and 'I can't drink I believed
the whole bottle'

the ocean shredded
by jet-ski boymen . . .
the biding waves waving

a mother's weary
smile, watching her son lob stones
into the sea

days and days
of summer rain;
it's the sea we breathe

the discos done,
owl and sea help themselves
to the night that's theirs

barbie smoke, crickets –
and it's begun again
'to get late early'

the seafront flags
winnowed, by autumn,
to ragged halves

high tide too
in every dinghy laid up
against the storms

black Lab puppy
dodging the waves; there's time, still,
to outlive a dog

THE COMMONS

She seems to me still the very spirit of the commons. Often to be seen striding the roads of Gower – in Fedora-style hat atop long, black, silver-streaked hair, shawl the colour of winter bracken, voluminous skirt and black leather boots – Mrs Hearn would find her way to our door, at Kilvrough Park Farm, about a kilometre south-west of Fairwood Common, two or three times a year. My mother would welcome her in and invite her to take a seat, but, always declining the offer of a chair, she'd simply squat on the kitchen floor, her basket beside her, and puff away on her briar – just like an old squaw, it seemed to us boys, obsessed as we were with cowboys and Injuns. She smelled of rain, woodsmoke and sweat. But, in spite of her deeply lined and weather-burnished face, she wasn't that old. Not so long ago, we knew, she'd lost her daughter, aged about twenty, to polio – a legendarily beautiful girl by the name of Fairy.

The purpose of her visit, amid the tale-telling and sipping of tea laced with whiskey, was trade. Among the merchandise in her cloth-covered basket would be a couple of boiling pans, made by the men of the tribe, shoelaces, and clothes pegs fashioned from two sticks whittled to shape and bound together with bands of tin. My mother could always be relied on to purchase a few pegs and then, as Mrs Hearn prepared to leave, to part with the requested 'rusty bacon' (from the hams hanging overhead) and some 'mouldy tea' – tea being, still, a rationed commodity.

The Hearns (or Herons as they were sometimes known) lived on Fairwood Common, just south of Three Crosses. Their encampment, in the lee of some coal tips (since removed), was for years a colourful landmark, with its tents, traditional wagons or 'vardos', wood fires, skewbald horses, and children running around with yapping dogs at their heels. Modern caravans and flatbeds may gradually have superseded the vardos and horses, but Romanies through and through the Hearns remained, held in general affection by the surrounding 'gorgio' community. In springtime the encampment would thin out, as

many of them left to spend the summer months with another branch of the tribe at Kilgetty, near Tenby. It was usually, therefore, during the winter that Mrs Hearn called on us (she relished the warmth from our kitchen stove after the walk across the common). When she did eventually become too old and infirm to do her rounds, my mother received a note from one of her family saying that although she was no longer fit enough to pay us a visit, she would still be able to collect her Christmas box from Dunvant post office – which my mother duly despatched.

The Gypsies, who disappeared from Fairwood decades ago, clearly felt at home on Verras Moor, as the common used to be known, whereas the 'gorgios', then as now, rarely ventured more than a few metres from the commons' roadside verges, if they troubled at all to park their cars and take in the view. In spite of the Countryside and Rights of Way Act 2000, which granted access to all registered common land, you rarely see walkers setting forth confidently across the common, no doubt because it's known to have precariously boggy patches and also, perhaps, because of some residual suspicion of Verras Moor's reputation, long before the construction of the turnpike roads, as the haunt of robbers.

At weekends in the 1950s and '60s, dozens of learner drivers used to practise on an unused expanse of airport runway beside the A4118 south Gower road, plane-spotters used to spot, and Mr Softee would do a brisk trade in ice creams. But the local authority, which was given Fairwood Common by the Lord of Kilvrough Manor in 1935, placed barriers against such access, and some other commons, such as Clyne, were (controversially) fenced off. In contrast with the much frequented clifftops, the 'inland' commons are generally ignored by natives and visitors alike; but they are, literally, a central feature of Gower's identity, and it's impossible to conceive of the peninsula without them.

Some 70 sq. kms of the peninsula – about half of its surface – comprise unfertile common land, in 24 distinct parcels and of 3 main types: the sea-cliff commons of the south, the marshes of the north, and the inland commons, across which most of us speed in our cars, paying scant attention to the gorse, the dancing bog cotton, the bracken, the purple moor grass, the wind-tousled herds of wild ponies . . . and slowing down only to let some sheep or lumbering cow cross the road in front of us.

these June grasses
dusted with rain – I need no god
to find them holy

The big inland commons – Fairwood, Clyne, Pengwern, Welsh Moor – lie mostly on Millstone Grit, a poorly drained mudstone base grudgingly disposed to vegetal proliferation. The commons' wet, if not waterlogged, soils are dense, cold and unaerated – conditions which tend to retard the breakdown of plant and animal matter, resulting in the build-up of undecayed peat and increasing acidity. As the turf on Clyne golf course suggests, however, some drier tracts of common are improvable, and certain farms adjoining the commons have benefited from incorporating marginal land and turning it into productive fields. But the effort has generally been deemed not worthwhile, so that the commons still have much the same boundaries as they have had for thousands of years.

When the Norman invaders annexed south Gower and drove the natives into what became Gower *Wallicana* (Welsh Gower), the commons acted as a line of demarcation between the two peoples, and they are the most obvious relics of the medieval pattern of land use to be seen in today's landscape. They may have acted as neutral territory between the two cultures, but they weren't exactly no-man's-land. All common land has an owner: if not 'the lord of the manor', then, in Gower's case, the National Trust, the City and County of Swansea, the Duke of Beaufort, and a company of commoners formed in 1974 as the Llangennith Manors. The feudal or manorial system established by the Normans ensured that the commons – or 'manorial waste', as they termed non-cultivable land – played an important role in the farming system, particularly for the grazing of livestock. It has remained the case into modern times, that in order to qualify – as a 'commoner' – for grazing rights, a farmer has to own land adjacent to the common. A commoner had other rights too, rarely invoked these days: estover (to take firewood and bracken for fuel and bedding), turbary (to dig peat), piscary (to fish the streams), pannage (to feed pigs on acorn and beech mast), coire (to take stone) and 'common in soil' (to take gravel and sand).

To the passing motorist, the commons may look wild and untended, but for hundreds of years they have been in the stewardship of Gower's commoners, who number today about 500. The hand of the Gower Commoners Association, which was founded in 1947, may be seen in such features as cattle grids and fences, and in the widespread 'bracken bashing' that takes place in the summer in order to promote better grazing. Bracken is also

**though still some sun –
also, now, blackberries
and crickets**

harvested to make a peat-free compost sold as Gower Soil Conditioner. Less apparent is the association's work 'behind the scenes', such as rotating the stallions among the commons' herds of ponies, to avoid in-breeding and the production of poor-quality ponies that may be fit only for dog meat.

Although the commons seem unchanging from one year to the next, quite significant changes are detectable from decade to decade. As on common land throughout Wales, overgrazing has been responsible for the encroachment of bracken, bramble, gorse and rushes. Since the 1970s, the eastern reaches of Fairwood and the south-western portion of Clyne, where alder and sallows have survived the busy incisors of sheep, are well on the way to becoming the kind of scrubby woodland that would come to dominate the commons were it not for the presence of cattle, sheep and ponies.

The most dramatic changes, of course, have been the result of direct human intervention. The extreme circumstances of the Second World War saw a boggy swathe of Fairwood Common turned, within a year, into an aerodrome for fighter planes of the Allied forces, using thousands of tons of industrial slag from the Lower Swansea Valley to consolidate the runways. When it was turned into a civil airport in the 1950s, it was decreed that 'if the enclosed area ceases to be used as an aerodrome, it shall revert to an open space'. Notwithstanding such good intentions, in the late 1960s a madcap scheme briefly surfaced for turning Fairwood Common into an industrial estate, and a few years ago the local authority gave itself permission to build four massive hangars at the airport, each of them – as the Gower Society noted – 'bigger than anything built in Gower since the Norman conquest's castles'.

Other threats to the commons include uncontrolled fires, flytipping, and four-wheel-drive vehicles and scramble motorbikes, which have caused considerable damage to fragile turf systems, particularly those of Cefn Bryn. Roaring through the bracken in what seems like an unassuageable rage, these lost boy-men (of the tribe whose 'other car' is probably a jet ski) seem as oblivious as the champions of industrial estates and giant hangars to the ensorcelling music of skylark and curlew.

****

PIG-KILLING DAY

I watched from the bedroom, all sound
from out there jammed by the music
that boomed inside.
                              Then up
from the beech-tops the rooks
unfurled, hung streaming
through dull white sky,
          till a peace below
                    drew them filtering back
and someone turned down the broadcast.

They dragged her from the trailer
like some damaged drunk, his
nakedness snarled with red string,
and in the outhouse where
we'd stewed her spuds, they
hooked her up, paunch taut
for the knife's first nagging.

Heads above bowls
crossed the yard
                         all day
as they scraped and scalded,
hacked and subtracted, slowly
spreading the room with pig.

The kitchen by evening was plump
with faggots and strange other
pieces.

All that remained
of the pig I'd known lay uncurled
in the coal hod, brightened with dust.
They said me goodnight, with their
clean hands brushed me . . .

We ate well of the pig, she
lasted us months,
                          though for days
I preferred to ride on the tractor, shy
of the trailer, the death
  it brought home.

WILLY HARRY

He and his men, from a child's viewpoint, were giants who bestrode the forests and rickyards of Gower – with spectacular machines at their command that seemed to make the whole planet tremble.[1]

They came once in the depths of a '50s winter to take timber from our wood, with a saw-bench the size of an aircraft carrier, a traction engine, two low-slung Fordson tractors – and a will unthwarted by any blizzard, injury or mechanical hitch. When the steering on one of the Fordsons failed, they simply manhandled, booted and rammed the front wheels until the tractor took the desired route through the Somme-like mud. In the stillness of a Sunday, the trench-scarred woodland seemed to reel from the week's campaign, a strange silence defined by the dune of sawdust built up beneath that jagged disc of steel.

Another winter's task was thrashing. Reaped and bound into sheaves in late summer, the corn crop would be piled for a few months into ricks the size of an outhouse, until the blustery morning when Willy and crew rumbled into the yard with traction engine, baler and his red-and-yellow thrashing machine. A spanner, a few words, then the drive-wheels would turn and, clacking and whirring, the belts would start to build the pulse. With a string at each knee to prevent vermin from fleeing up their trouser legs, the men piked the rick sheaf by sheaf into the wooden maw of the thrasher, where the grain was shaken free of the straw and the straw relayed to the baling machine. To my brother and me, the mice were Germans plundering the farm's treasure, or pink nests of infidel Injuns. Heroic under the arms of men sweeping wheat through grey skies, we'd stamp on the babies and flick them half crushed to the cats below, or chase the grown ones with pitchforks and pin them, writhing, to the cobbled yard.

How we were hoisted to fame by the legends spun over midday's ham, cider and tea. And how we cringed at bedtime from the day's bloody deeds, both of us wanting, from now on, to take the Indians' part – for the world, it seemed, was crawling with cowboys.

at home too

a buzzard's cry, the soughing of firs

remind me of home

sunned earth fizzing

with rumours of barley

as the rain sinks home

---

[1] There were three main families involved in traction-engine contracting in Gower: the Gordons of Llanrhidian, the Greenings of Killay and the Harrys of Cilibion.

last year's leaves –
a bushy oak rustling
in icy winds.

The last time I saw Willy, in the 1970s, he was gusting down High Street like a snatch of old rick. He was sure of it, he told me, sure: steam was going to come again; he was calling back from the yards of Wales all his old engines to power once more the saw-bench and the thrasher. Swansea's shoppers walked wide of the dribbled chin and those spacey, blue, blood-rimmed eyes. Winnowing today's unmemorable chaff from the abundant grain of yesterday, he was back where I remembered him, uprooting forests and turning to a hurricane the autumn sleep of oats and barley. But time was money; he couldn't stop: he'd an engine up in Penllergaer Woods, there was work to be done. Steam, yes, was coming back, back to redeem us from the terrible folly of oil and electric.

I heard of him a year or two later, trammelled in the depths of age's forest, attempting, with pan and spatula, to fry an entire ham. Of Willy thereafter I heard no more.

****

PLANTS

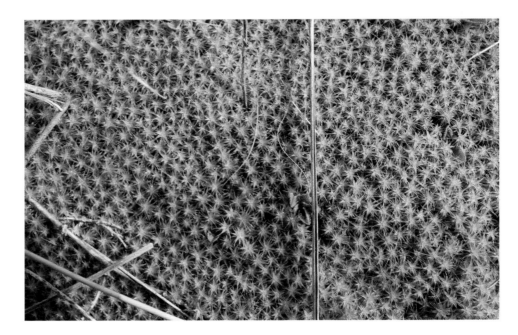

BLOSSOM TIME, MUMBLES

It comes round again, and who in the whole
of this half-done world isn't wet
between the mind's legs
with the woods-mulched garlic, bum-fluff greens
and these undomesticating bombs of sunflesh,
here today, gone
with the clichés of the haiku boys?

Cherry white, cherry pink, the snow winds'
ambush, every April of my life
you've sung me into May,
and every April I've ached
for the time and chutzpah
to sift among the blown petals of speech
for the phonemes to shape you a bowl of praise.

But always I've been busy, always too fussed
with defrosting the fridge, or
the comet-of-a-lifetime . . .
And they're gone, the blossoms,
gone in a night, before the ice in my fridge
has turned to slush . . .

And ah well, I've said, there's always
again, and when the weather's right
I'll amble a bit, and sit on a stone
and take purposeful note . . .

The late snows are melting on Carreg y Fan,
and again is here: blossoms out, shirts off,
the first legs of the year
driving both shirted and shirtless wild . . .
and – what's this? – the alleged poet
is busier than a busted bee
exercising the goldfish?

This April the blossoms have been saying to me:
'What kind, gwboi, what kind
of a presumptuous, nervy bastard are you
that you dare to dream
you'll be present here in a year's turning
– for yet again your pen to ignore us?
Live the now, boy blossom, and finish
your sentence.'

And they unbury for the baby
a morning perhaps or an afternoon
when I gazed from my pram
on a quilted great arc of flouncy sky –
the pink of it, the blue, the necessary crow.

But nothing done, for the forty-seventh time.
And all I dare say, as the storm-troops drive
the last of the lost into the sea, is
'Same time next year?'

INDUSTRIAL GOWER

Few explorers of Britain's first Area of Outstanding Natural Beauty realise the extent to which they are moving through a post-industrial landscape. Farming, with associated activities such as weaving, corn-milling and blacksmithing, has obviously been, for centuries, the peninsula's staple industry. But hidden (or ignored) on cliffsides, in valleys, on commons and in certain built-up areas – are hints and rumours of a largely unsuspected range of industries – from coal, iron, silver and lead mining to the quarrying and burning of limestone, brass and copper smelting, tinplate production, shipbuilding and brick-making – some of which have had a profound influence on the making of Gower.

If peninsular Gower is defined roughly as the land that lies west of a ragged line drawn from Blackpill in the south-east to Gowerton in the north-east – along which, sooner or later, the sea will find its way, making once again an island of Gower – then any of the landward 'gateways to Gower' will take you across its defunct industrial belt, which curved westward at Gowerton to take in much of north Gower, reaching almost as far as Llanrhidian (in the 16th century, coal was mined as far west as Landimore). Apart from some terraced workers' housing at places such as Blackpill, Killay, Dunvant, Gowerton and, above all, Penclawdd, there are few obvious clues to the region's industrial past.

But lurking among the trees, bushes, fern and bramble that have triumphantly re-conquered much of this formerly productive terrain are intriguing relics of what, for hundreds of years, was a crucible of industrial activity.

To walk through the densely wooded Clyne Valley Country Park, between Blackpill and Killay, if you know where to look and what to look for, is to encounter a fossilised industrial landscape – which is in a far better state of preservation than the more famous industrial environment of the Lower Swansea Valley.

From at least the early 14th century until the 1920s, coal was mined here. The remains of scores of pits, waste tips and associated chunks of machinery are still to be found, from

deep mines such as Coed yr Ysgol – whose collapsed shaft, south-east of the disused bridge at the Killay end of the park, has provided local bike boys with a thrilling 'plunge of death' – to the smaller scale bell pits which are dotted around the valley, particularly on the western side of the foot-and-bike path.

Easy to identify before springtime's resurgence of bracken, bell pits were primitive coal workings formed by miners digging out a hole a little over a metre in diameter and three metres deep, then belling out at the bottom as far as they dared without bringing the roof down on top of them. There are over 250 bell pits in Clyne Valley, and they are identifiable as mounds of waste on the lower side of shallow, basin-shaped sinks, sometimes water-filled. There were slant or drift mines too: a good example survives towards the southern end of the popular fishing pool that is skirted by the bike path, although it is grilled and padlocked against entry.

Other Clyne industries – with associated canals, railways, tramways, cart tracks and leats (for water power) – included iron mining and smelting, copper smelting, charcoal production, naptha and cellulose extraction, and brick-making. North-east of the bridge at the Killay end of the main path is a tree-shaded pond and the remains of the last of Clyne's brickworks which, shortly before it closed in about 1950, was producing 75,000 bricks a week. The buildings have been demolished, apart from odd fragments of concrete flooring, but there are several mounds – disguised by moss – of thousands of warped, bulbous, doubled, broken or otherwise misshapen bricks which have been rejected. They are stamped variously 'Evans-Bevan Ltd / Clyne Works / Killay', 'Clyne / Killay', or simply 'Killay'.

Disguise of a different sort shrouds the original purpose of what has been castellated to look like a Gothic tower, in the south-west corner of the park, a couple of hundred metres north of Clyne Castle. Neither a medieval ruin nor an indulgent landowner's romantic folly, the tower was built as an exhaust stack for noxious fumes from the arsenic works a couple of hundred metres down the slope, and later turned into a Gothic pavilion. It was connected to the works by a flue tunnel, caved-in sections of which lead you, through scrubby undergrowth, to the (surprisingly substantial) ivy-clad remains of the Clyne Wood Arsenic Works: the stump of another stack with a sawn-off tree trunk sticking out of its stonework,

bluebells, garlic –

and a whiff of tobacco

the smoker gone

the remains of furnaces encrusted with crystallised arsenic, flue labyrinths, an office block with fireplaces, windows, doorways and rotting lintels, lengths of wall as high in places as six or nine metres. Built in the mid 1840s, the works fell into disuse about fifteen years later, probably because of its proximity to the country mansions of members of the powerful Morris and Vivian industrial dynasties, who could tolerate a few coal mines in the valley beneath them but not the highly poisonous arsenic fumes that were gusting from those stacks. That so much of the works has survived into the present is due partly to its subsequent re-use as hay sheds and partly to the dense foliage on the slope around it, which has rendered it largely invisible and relatively inaccessible. As 'the only eighteenth-century or early nineteenth-century works in the former world centre of the non-ferrous smelting industry to preserve remains of its productive plant' – to quote John Newman – it's an internationally important site; but 'the authorities', as usual, seem oblivious.

Coal was the catalyst for Clyne's industries, just as it was for the industrial development of the Dunvant–Gowerton–Penclawdd tract. Rich seams of a wide range of coals, from bituminous to anthracitic, outcrop in a continuous band from Blackpill to Wernffrwd, just west of Penclawdd.

To the Normans, intent on appropriating the most productive farmland, north-east Gower was the badlands, and the natives were welcome to the region's meagre pickings. With plentiful supplies of wood, the Normans and the Anglo-Normans would have had no interest in mining coal. But by the 17th century, the north-east's substantial coal reserves were proving increasingly valuable, advantage being taken of their proximity to what was once a deepwater anchorage, before the river Llwchwr changed course in the later 1800s and accretions of silt obstructed the approaches to Penclawdd. But there were two major disadvantages to what were heavily faulted seams: their tendency to slope northwards at a steep angle, forcing the miner to pursue his seam downwards, uncertain as to how soon his efforts would prove unprofitable; and their perennial wetness, with a propensity to sometimes disastrous flooding. Penclawdd mines were said to be 'like the Indian Ocean underground'. And some mines were literally submarine undertakings: miners working beneath the estuary were frequently unnerved to hear the sea moving a short distance above their heads.

the rains,

in breeze-rushed leaves,

transformed

COAL

White world, grey endless sky –
the birds hunched and starving,
　　our pipes frozen.

Of the sun there is nothing.

Yet when I scoop up
some snow, when I take in my hand
a coal fallen from the heaped bucket
I balance on my palm
the history of rivers, I am in touch
with dark original forests.

Branches of coal
spread out beneath us,

a language of the sun,
　　locked
　　by the ancient trees in their cells,
and translated again
　　by the green sun
　　that goes whispering
　　through sinew and bone.

With deadened fingers
we build up the grate.

Seedlings of flame

Shift and flicker: fire awakening,
fire remembering in its first tongue
the journey from sun to greening earth.

It fills up our faces,
and the rivers of cold
chase through our bodies

    to spill from chasms just north
    of the base of the spine.

we do not see

til flight tilts them sunward –

oystercatchers

The fragmented, unpredictable seams of north-east Gower tended to favour small-scale operations, initially by farmers and their farm hands, venturing no deeper with their 'crop holes' than could be managed with picks and shovels. As in Clyne, there were bell pits too, the remains of which can be seen in the Morlais Valley below Cilonnen. But there were more purposeful undertakings, with workforces, buildings and tramways: by the mid 19th century, there were two dozen such ventures around Penclawdd. The extension of the railway from Gowerton to Penclawdd and eventually to Llanmorlais, between 1866 and 1877, revitalised industry in the area, but the collieries declined after 1920. By 1950, coalmining in north Gower – which in 1913 employed 1,636 men – had virtually ceased. There are still traces of the industry: depressions and undulations in certain fields, such as those at Penllwyn-Robert; ivy-clad pit-head ruins and tramway embankments; the remains of smaller spoil tips, the bigger ones – such as those on Fairwood Common, to the south of Three Crosses – having been removed during the post-Aberfan restitutions of the late '60s and early '70s. Such traces can take some finding, especially in summer. The most conspicuous relic of all, in a field at Caer Eithin about half a kilometre west of the Poundffald pub, is the Berthlwyd Colliery Company's massive engine house, built in the early 1900s from Killay brick and local sandstone. In a neighbouring field, there's a roofless but thick-walled and curiously windowless building which turns out to be the colliery's explosives store.

North Gower's abundance of coal encouraged the growth of other significant industries. On the eastern approach to Penclawdd, on the marsh opposite the rugby club, there's an assembly of chunky 'monoliths' which looks as if a gorsedd circle has enjoyed an encounter with Salvador Dali. These knobbly extrusions, ideal scratching posts for the marsh's sheep, are slag waste from the copper smelting works, which began operations in 1790, on a site previously occupied by a brass works. Copper, in spite of severe fluctuations in its fortunes here, played a decisive role in the growth of industrial Penclawdd, which became Gower's biggest village – growth dependent for some time, shamefully, on the production of copper 'rods' and horse-shoe shaped bronze 'manillas' used in bartering for slaves in west Africa. The plant, which latterly smelted lead and silver, closed in the 1880s; near the sewage works, there are one or two fragments of original wall.

Penclawdd's copper ore came – by ship – from Cornwall and Anglesey, and its zinc and lead from Pembrokeshire. Today's network of shallow muddy creeks through marshland that comes right up to the sea wall would seem to make a nonsense of Penclawdd's claims to have been a thriving port and to have had a shipbuilding tradition – which indeed it had, between 1829 and 1938, producing vessels as large as 30-ton sloops and 80-ton schooners. One of the few mementoes of the village's seafaring past is a low, bushy promontory, about 100 m long, pushing out into the marshland at Abercedi, a few hundred metres east of the slag monoliths. This is the Penclawdd canal dock (*c.* 1812), terminus of the short-lived Gowerton to Penclawdd canal, which was later overlain, along much of its course, by the railway (which itself closed in 1957, and whose track-bed is now a foot-and-bike path). The overgrown canal basin, extending about two thirds down the quay, is still discernible, as is some of the stonework of the eastside wharf, along with the pond where water was dammed for scouring the dock; it is host these days to a magnificent stand of bulrushes. The coming of the railway and the relentless silting of the – now far distant – channel had nullified the dock by 1870. At the dock's seaward end, a leggy hawthorn, much trodden round its base by itchy sheep, stands lone sentinel.

Another major Penclawdd industry was tinplate production, which began in 1872 and at its peak employed 600 men. Like other tinplate enterprises, it was hard hit by the McKinley tariff of 1891, which severely curtailed exports to the United States. What became the Gower Iron and Tinplate Works closed in 1895; its buildings were dismantled two years later.

Other Penclawdd industries included the production of chemicals, arsenic and mineral paints. Various fields in the locality with names such as Cae yr Odyn (kiln field) testify to the use of kilns for lime-burning, brick-making (with clay from local coal pits) and the production of pottery.

There was invariably a boom-and-bust pattern to the development of industry in north Gower, with farming, fishing and cockling providing an invaluable mainstay at times of industrial retrenchment. Although the community that industry created here from about 1600 onwards had – and still has – much in common with other communities of industrial Wales, north-east Gower has always been, uniquely, a country and maritime coalfield with a distinctive and coherent culture – predominantly Welsh-speaking, Nonconformist in

from the pub sways

a choir, tied and suited,

on a cloud of aftershave

religion and Liberal or socialist in politics – that contrasts conspicuously with the Anglophone, Anglican and Conservative inclinations of many in south Gower.

Penclawdd's south-coast *doppelgänger*, in some ways, is Mumbles, which for all its fashionability and high property prices still has a residual, if diminishing, working class. At the heart of the village – as distinct from its moneyed outer reaches – are tightly packed terraces built originally for quarrymen, miners and fishermen, reminding us that the village's original *raison d'être* was not leisure and tourism but industry. The Mumbles train,[1] famous as the world's first passenger-carrying railway, was conceived by industrialists, mainly for transporting minerals from Mumbles and Clyne to the industries of the Lower Swansea Valley. Many of those domiciled in Mumbles worked in the industries of Clyne; others worked closer to home, Mumbles being, for much of the 19th century, one vast limestone quarry. Iron ore was also mined here (and, in a small way, between Ram's Tor and Rotherslade), from the Roman period until the end of the 19th century. A blood-red seam of haematite ran across Mumbles Hill, from opposite what is now the Knab Rock car park – where there is still a deep, red gash in the cliff – to Limeslade, where it peters out pinkly on the east side of the beach. Its extraction left a trench across the hill, most of which was backfilled with limestone from the cavern blasted out of Mumbles Hill to make an underground sewage works in the 1930s.

Gower's iron oxides are thought to have derived from water percolating through a pre-existing cover of iron-rich desert sandstones of the Triassic (or early dinosaur) period. A remnant of that cover exists at Port Eynon: its red ochre was used not only to stain the bones of 'the Red Lady of Paviland' (29,900 years ago) but also as the basis of the Great Western Railway's livery of brown and ochre. The ochre was mined and exploited commercially as a paint pigment from the 1690s onwards.

An important Port Eynon industry was salt extraction – extensive remains of its salthouse are still to be seen at the sea's edge. There were salthouses also at Crofty, Oystermouth and, in Swansea, at Fabian's Bay (which was obliterated when work began on the eastside docks in 1879).

Other industrial activities in south Gower include a small (and disputed) lead mining venture in Bishopston Valley, and a much more extensive lead and silver enterprise at

---

[1] The Mumbles Railway was destroyed in 1961 in what has been described as an act of 'heritage homicide'.

nearby Hareslade and Brandy Cove, based on the mining of galena. All that remains, as you walk down to Brandy Cove today, are the ruins of a blacksmith's shop at the edge of a field. But in the mid 19th century, the little valley would have been a hive of dirty and smoky activity, with half a dozen mine shafts, winding gear, spoil tips, a coal-fired boiler with engine shaft and associated coal and ash tips, a lead works with ore-crushing machinery, tramways and water channels. All visible remains were cleared, apart from that blacksmith's shed, towards the end of the last century.

If coal, the dominant industry of north Gower, has left few traces in the landscape, the same cannot be said of the south coast's dominant industry, limestone. Its extraction has left permanent, though generally well-disguised, scars on the landscape. The closure in the 1980s of Gower's last working limestone quarry, Barlands at Kittle, marked the end of what had been an important industry, in which individual quarries often produced limestone of different qualities to serve different purposes. From Mumbles to Rhosili, there were quarries on all the major headlands, altering the appearance of whole cliffsides, and in places such as Barlands and Mumbles half a hill or more has been removed: in Mumbles, for instance, an entire housing estate squats in the vast arena blasted out of Colts Hill by one of Gower's biggest quarrying concerns.

Many hundreds were employed in quarrying, transporting and burning the stone, in the numerous kilns – most of them built between 1750 and 1850 – that are still to be seen along the roadsides of southern Gower, those roads themselves, like most of the older houses, having been constructed of limestone. Lime, produced by burning the stone at 1000°C, was – and still is – in regular use in agriculture as a soil 'sweetener', rendering acid ground more fertile. It has had many other uses: as a component of mortar and plaster and of farmhouse fuel, a whitewash, a disinfectant, a seed dressing, an ant killer, a purifying element in gas and sewage systems, a tanning agent, the raw material of asphalt and breeze-blocks. It also played a crucial role as a flux in the revolutionary iron-making process devised by Sidney Gilchrist Thomas at Blaenavon in the 1870s; the 'basic slag' which was a by-product of that process was then returned to the land as an agricultural fertilizer.

What industry survives in today's Gower is confined largely to the Crofty Industrial Estate, inflicting minimal disturbance on that sugar-coated substitute industry, tourism.

after the rain, more drizzle –

this weather melts no jellyfish

It is, no doubt, generally to the good that arsenic fumes no longer gust through the trees at Clyne and that the dumping of coal spoil on the fields around Penclawdd long ago ceased. Work in Gower's 'traditional' industries was invariably hard and unhealthy, and the land too suffered degradation and pollution. There would be an outcry today were some entrepreneur to propose, say, the resumption of quarrying at Ilston. But with the slate wiped so seemingly clean of those industries, I can't help feeling a perverse sense of loss. I well remember docking mangolds on a frosty morning at Kilvrough, or sweating under the cosh of the hay harvest in June (my least favourite job on the farm), and hearing the shrill of the siren at Ilston quarry or Barlands – thirty seconds precisely, then, following the bump of the blast, three short wails, and all would be clear. I'd feel a sense of continuity between my labours in the field and those of the quarryman[2] less than a mile distant – both of us engaged in useful, necessary work. It's harder to share with the transient consumers of Gower's 'scenery' a comparable sense of coherence and purpose.

****

[2] Many a Gower man in the past was both quarryman and farm labourer.

THE GOWER SHOW

The Gower Agricultural Show, which marked its 100th anniversary in 2005, is the biggest event in the peninsula's farming calendar, attracting crowds of 10,000 every first Sunday in August to its traditional home in Penrice Castle's stately parkland. Since the sudden – and permanent – closure in 2001 of the weekly livestock market at Gowerton as a result of the Britain-wide foot-and-mouth outbreak, the Gower Show is now the only opportunity that Gower farming people have to assemble as a community.

For most show-goers, including thousands from Swansea and further afield, it's about the busiest and most beguiling one-day event in the west, but for Gower folk – Beynons, Tuckers, Richardses, Gordons, Bevanses, Harrys, Waterses – catching up with all the gossip since last they gathered here in strength, it can be in addition a quietly poignant experience. In a world of whimsical unpredictability, the Gower Show seems, from one year to the next, unchanging and unchangeable. The sun, strange to say, invariably shines; there's that scintillating glimpse of Oxwich Bay beyond the castle ruins to the south of the site; there's the sweet savour, always, of trodden grass, and there are oases of shade beneath sycamore, oak and beech; to the north, there's the perennial, reassuring presence of Cefn Bryn's ferny ridge. But all are subject to life's seismic alterations, and the reliable solidities of the Gower Show may console as readily as they may provoke a sting of *hiraeth* for what has been and gone since the tribe last rallied on this tented sward: a parent's death, perhaps, or a marriage gone mysteriously to seed, or those six prime acres reluctantly sold to pay off seemingly insurmountable debts.

The August 1939 show, the *Evening Post* declared – days before World War II broke out – 'was in no way affected by affairs in Europe'. And the centenary show in 2005 – which lured me back, like a prodigal son, after an absence of nearly forty years – seemed in no way affected by affairs in Iraq, or anywhere else. As a rebellious youth, with a taste for long hair, red frock coats and the orgasmitudes of Jimi Hendrix, I grew impatient with blinkered

Gower conservatism, as I saw it: I wanted out and I stayed out, until I could return, a decade or so later, on my own terms. Now, in my mid fifties, I was ready to renew my acquaintance with the Gower Show (which I had shunned partly, indeed, because of its relocation, from 1987 to 2001, to the banal flatlands of Swansea Airport). All, as I approached the showground in my brother Martyn's four-by-four, seemed much as I'd left it in the 1960s. It did indeed feel a bit like a homecoming, and if, surely, that old conservatism still prevailed, I could agree by now to differ with it and to accept that, in a benign domestic application, it had at least kept this august show on the road.

The show has been woven into the fabric of Jenkins family life for generations. Between 1906 and 1925, it was held on alternate years at Kilvrough, on land which in 1920, following the break-up of the Kilvrough Estate, became the property of my grandfather, T.E. (Tom) Jenkins. During the 1920s, he was the show secretary; so too, later on, were my father Rowland, my brother Martyn and my sister Carey. On show days, my mother Gloria used to get up at 'sparrow fart' (as she used to say) to arrange the flowers in the members' tent. My own pre-show job, as a boy – and under the demanding supervision of Gower Davies, the local postman – was to help set out the trestle tables in the flower tent, the biggest on the field, and to cover them with newsprint donated by the *Evening Post*. I also had to dig out a trench for the women's toilets in a roofless corner of the old castle, and to help erect over the trench a superstructure made of planks and sacking, which would provide a degree of (visual) privacy for visitors to our elongated thunder box. (Today's conveniences comprise a couple of dozen unisex portaloos arranged, not too far from the beer tent, in a large semicircle.) On the day itself, in addition to competing in the horse classes, there would be stewarding duties and the running of errands, which would work up a thirst for underage shandies.

I leave my brother among the horseboxes, harnessing his hackney for the driving class, and, as I head towards the action, it's my sister's voice that rings out over the showground – 'RP' posh (today) and expletive-free – from her announcer's box beside the main ring. 'A big round of applause, ladies and gentlemen, please, for the best small hunter of fourteen two hands . . .', followed shortly by 'Would the parents of ten-year-old Daniel Roberts from Treboeth, who has lost his mum and dad, please come and fetch him from the

commentators' box . . .' As it was, is now and ever shall be, I find myself musing, half expecting any minute to bump into stalwarts of Gower Shows past: show director, Home Farm tenant and genial, gangly Yorkshireman Alan Turnbull, with bowler hat and shooting stick; the portly and pukkah Christopher Methuen-Campbell, who inherited the Penrice Estate from his grandmother, Lady Blythswood, in 1958; champion ploughman Jack Tanner, with the Brylcreemed mohawk that was then the manly norm; Colonel Frank 'Monocle' Morgan in plus fours; Colonel C. Rosser John, with a handlebar moustache as white as his champion Welsh mountain ponies; the gruff-and-no-nonsense RSPCA Inspector Jim Nash, doubling on show day as an announcer; the hulking police Superintendent J. Hewlett; Dr Bill Moreton of Reynoldston, with thumbstick, military 'tache, and a right eyebrow whose quizzical elevation had the power to screw boyish lesser breeds straight into the turf; and his neighbours, Dr Bill and Molly Rees-Jones, my parents' rotund and jolly drinking pals. But they, and dozens more I could name, died years ago, and I find myself wandering round like a stranger in my own dream. I recognise no one, except the local undertaker – who's looking none too healthy himself.

Events in the main arena are not quite the attraction they used to be, when cars were allowed to park at the ring's edge. You'd aim to arrive at the showground at about 8 a.m., to avoid the traffic jams that topped and tailed show day, and to have any prospect of parking up against the ropes. Once you'd bagged a space, the roof and bonnet of your vehicle would serve as an ideal grandstand and picnicking platform. The climax was always the horse jumping, when the biggest names in British show jumping – Harry Llewellyn, Alan Oliver, Pat Smythe, David Broome – would thrill capacity crowds jostling for space between the sunned metal of the ringside Land Rovers and saloons. These days, people sit on the straw bales around the ring largely because it's somewhere to sit, not because they are particularly enthralled by the horse classes and their arcane, chivalric procedures, which involve much touching and removing of judges' and competitors' bowlers, toppers and Panama hats. It used to be close to a mortal sin to enter the ring without headwear, and your jacket had to be done up with the middle button. 'Certain standards' seem still to apply in that department, but elsewhere informality rules. In the members' tent these days – flowerless, and fenced not with hurdles but with brash lengths of orange 'incident tape' – trainers, T-shirts and baseball caps have taken over from the bowlers, trilbies, waistcoats and gleaming brogues of yesteryear. There used to be a provocative tension between the dressiness and decorum of the members' tent and the gusto with which the members (much less bibulous today) knocked back the booze. My mother recalls one bumper session when she and friends were still clinking glasses at the bar as the tent was dismantled around them, the moon came up and the stars began to shine.

The showground's layout has changed little since the early 1930s. Its main artery is the asphalted drive which runs diagonally across the park, from the grand portals at the Home Farm crossroads down to the new 'castle' – a neo-classical villa of the 1770s – that nestles out of sight in the lee of its medieval predecessor. To the left, at the top of the field, are the sheep and cattle lines (no pigs these days). To the right, behind a 'street' of trade stands selling farm machinery and equipment, are the horse lines, with grooms grooming, dainty riding ponies daisy-cutting the grass with their oiled hooves, picnics with warm Chardonnay in sunny gaps between horseboxes, as winners toast their triumphs and losers bemoan corrupt adjudications . . . and, maybe, in the leathery, ammoniac half-light of the odd horsebox – who's to see, who's to know? – a fleeting snog. If you catch a smell of singeing hereabouts, it'll be someone burning off the long hairs of a horse's muzzle and chin with a taper or a candle – hair, in this milieu, whether human or animal, being an entity in need of strict control.

Under the sycamores nearby is a collection of old tractors and engines lovingly restored by Gower vintage engine enthusiasts. Some of these 'historic' tractors must have been the latest thing in agricultural technology when I first started coming to the show in the 1950s. Among them are an orange Allis Chalmers, looking like a metal ant, a small grey Ferguson, and a low-slung, heavy Fordson, whose exhaust fumes – generated by a mixture of petrol and TVO (tractor vaporising oil) – are hauntingly evocative of my childhood on the farm. I could sniff them for hours.

On the other side of the drive is the funfair, with its throbbing generators, helter-skelter, rides of death, shooting galleries and amplified pop. Elvis's 'Hound Dog' and 'Blue Suede Shoes' blare out as I wander among the high-tech attractions, looking in vain for the swingboats, coconut shies, roll-a-penny and hooplah stalls, and the wasp-attracting candyfloss spinners of simpler times, when a goldfish in a plastic bag would be as good a prize as any to take home from the Gower Show.

As a child, I had little interest in the business of the poultry, horticulture, bee-keeping and WI tents. But they, with the livestock exhibits, are at the heart of what an agricultural show is all about: food – whereas the limelight-hogging horse classes, since horses have virtually no productive role to play in agriculture, are chiefly displays of ego and vanity. There's no denying a modicum of ego in the competitive spirit that has inspired, say, these vast onions nestling on a bed of sawdust (they were mulched, surely, on rather more than pure modesty) or this totem pole of a leek or those tables groaning under the weight of wines, honeycombs, currant cakes, breads, jams, quiches and tarts. But it's ego that has combined with labour, skill and the raw ingredients of life – to produce things that are beautiful, useful and sustaining. These tents are a true celebration of agricultural productivity and of the community (or what remains of it) that keeps farming in Gower alive.

The old castle these days is out of bounds: 'Dangerous Ruin No Entry'. But I find it easy enough to drag open the gate that's slumped across the entrance and have a wander. Built in the 13th century and the largest of Gower's medieval castles, it's much bigger than I remember. Beyond its still formidable walls, the clamour of the show – my sister on the loudspeaker, the neighing of horses, the whistling from the sheepdog trials – is reduced to a murmur. The loudest sounds in this realm of bramble, dock and thistle are the breeze's siftings through tall grasses and the skreekings of crickets, those harbingers of autumn. Having stood for nearly 800 years, the castle will no doubt hold its ground for a few hundred more. Given the deepening crises in agriculture and the environment, the Gower Show, for all its resilient bravura, seems, in comparison, a more fragile construction.

****

STUD

They fancy you from New South Wales
to Kansas, wherever the cymric mane
deranges an horizon. Sun smashes
over that pampered hide, arched within
a bridle's bare control, as you shrug
the bit to be at the mare. Joy-kicks
rent with farts disrupt the clockwork stride
which spirits you – addict, professional –
to where those back legs, dropped for ease
in a tractor rut, are scuffing the earth.

Reins tight beneath her chin – her fidget
arrested by some fear of what her blood
has always known – she stares back towards you,
her juice beginning to bead in the dust.
Your muzzle bumps the place, you sniff
again to prompt the signalling screech,
the raised hoof's proposal of a fight.
Your scream curdles, you rush on, forelegs
hoop her round. Jaw viced on her withers,
eyes riveting space, you bore into sleekness.

As industries once harness you, so
now you tunnel beauty's fiscal mine.
The mare bunches into your thrust; all
of sound and silence warp to this apex.
Two, three, six times daily, quickening to
the jar of flood . . . And you drop
from her, just able to stand, as day-sounds
prick the tension. Hurried breaths platter
the grass, then it's back to the gloom,
another pedigree satisfied.

COAST

CHAIN HARROWS

Diesel taints the sweet stench
of grass and scabbed manure.
Steel's rush, permitting but
the tink of stone, drags hanks of couch

from the stale pasture: they loll
in the crosswind, a whispered hay.
Third gear work, this; enigma
to Gower's newer eyes, peering

from the roads at little more than
some kind of lawn effect.
The bed reversed for cleaner ground,
I speed in top, dung shrapnel

sketting the air. Glancing back
to keep aligned, I catch
within the harrows' dance a frenzy
of bone – the skeleton burst

of rabbit or lamb. Shards litter
a region of bruised grass
like the spray of feathers
where a fox has killed.

SELECT BIBLIOGRAPHY

Balchin, W.G.V. (ed.), *Swansea and its Regions*, University College of Swansea, 1971

Bowen, Dewi, *Ancient Siluria: its old stones and ceremonial sites*, Llanerch, 1992

Castles of Gower, The, The Gower Society, 2005

Cooper, R.N., *A Dark and Pagan Place, A History of Penclawdd and District, Gower, West Glamorgan*, Cowbridge, 1986

Davies, Brian E., *Mumbles and Gower Pubs*, Tempus, 2006

Davies, John, *A History of Wales*, Penguin Books, 2007

Davies, John, Jenkins, Nigel, Baines, Menna, Lynch, Peredur I., *The Welsh Academy Encyclopaedia of Wales*, University of Wales Press, 2008

Davies, Latimer, *Pennard and West Gower*, Carmarthen, 1928

Davies, Paul R., *Historic Gower*, Christopher Davies, 1986

Ferris, Paul, *Gower in History*, Armanaleg Books, 2009

Gabb, Gerald, *The Story of the Village of Mumbles*, D. Brown and Sons Limited, Cowbridge, 1986; *The Life and Times of the Swansea and Mumbles Railway*, D. Brown and Sons Limited, Cowbridge, 1987; *Swansea and its History*, Swansea, 2007

Gillham, Mary E., *The Natural History of Gower*, D. Brown & Sons, 1977

Gower (1948–), the journal of The Gower Society

Gwynn, David R., *A History of the Gower Show*, Gower Agricultural Society, 1990

Middleton-Jones, Howard, *A Journey through Gower*, Christopher Davies, 1991

Minhinnick, Robert (ed.), *Green Agenda*, Seren, 1994

Morris, Bernard, *The Castles of Gower*, The Gower Society, 1969

Mullard, Jonathan, *Gower*, Collins, 2006

Nield, Ted, 'Gower – Story and Structure: a field guide to the solid geology of the Gower Peninsula' (The Geological Society; http://www.geolsoc.org.uk/template.cfm?name=Gower1test)

Newman, John, *The Buildings of Wales: Glamorgan*, Penguin, 1995

Orrin, Geoffrey R., *The Gower Churches*, The Rural Deanery of West Gower, 1979

Penhallurick, Robert, *Gowerland and its language*, Peter Lang, 1994

Rees, David, *A Gower Anthology*, Christopher Davies, 1977

Roberts, Ann, *Estuary People* (2001) and *We'll Never Be Young Again* (2008), both self-published

Tucker, Horatio, *Gower Gleanings*, The Gower Society, 1951

Thomas, J. Mansel, *The Sea Beneath My Feet*, The Gower Society, 1981; *Yesterday's Gower*, Gomer Press, 1982

Thomas, N.L., *Of Swansea West: The Mumbles, Past and Present*, Swansea, 1978

Vaughan Thomas, Wynford, *Portrait of Gower*, Robert Hale, London, 1983

Vernacular Gower, The Gower Society, 2003

Wakelin, Peter and Griffiths, Ralph A. (eds.), *Hidden Histories: Discovering the Heritage of Wales*, Comisiwn Brenhinol Henebion Cymru/Royal Commission on the Ancient and Historical Monuments of Wales, 2008

Whittle, Elisabeth, *Glamorgan and Gwent*, Cadw, 1992

Williams, Pat, *One Hundred Years of the Gower Show*, The Gower Agricultural Society, 2006

NOTES ON PHOTOGRAPHS

ACKNOWLEDGEMENTS

Among the many people whose memories, suggestions and practical assistance have been invaluable in the writing of this book, I am particularly grateful to (in alphabetical order) John Davies (the historian), Steve Dubé, Martyn Jenkins (my brother), Alan Kellermann, Carey Knox (my sister), Danny McCarroll, Gloria McLeod (my mother), Helle Michelsen, Elizabeth A. Walker (Collections Manager/Curator of Palaeolithic & Mesolithic Archaeology, National Museum Wales), Noel Witts (my cousin) and ever-helpful staff at Mumbles Library and the library of Swansea University. I thank my *compañera* Margot Morgan for her encouragement and her many helpful suggestions, in addition to her company on numerous Gower walks.

A particular debt of gratitude is owed to everyone at Gomer, especially Francesca Rhydderch who first suggested this book, many years ago, and who edited it with her usual (exemplary) diligence and flair, and Rebecca Ingleby Davies, the book's creative and resourceful designer.

I am grateful to the editors of *Roundyhouse* and *Planet: The Welsh Internationalist* for publishing earlier versions of, respectively, 'Willy Harry' and 'Farms', and to the editors of *Cambria* and *New Welsh Review* for publishing preview extracts from this book. Most of the haiku (the short, generally three-line poems) are taken from my two haiku collections, *Blue* (2002) and *O For a Gun* (2007), both of them published by Planet Books of Aberystwyth. The longer poems come from my collections *Acts of Union: Selected Poems 1974–1989* (1990), *Ambush* (1998) and *Hotel Gwales* (2006), all published by Gomer. Both Planet and Gomer are gratefully acknowledged.

****

GOWER

Llwchwr Estuary

Llwchwr

Whiteford
Point

Gowerton

Penclawdd

Three Crosses

The Marshes

Welsh Moor

Swansea

Burry
Holms

Cilifor
Top

Llanmadoc
Hill

Weobley Castle

Broad Pool

Pengwern + Fairwood
Commons

Clyne Valley

Arthur's Stone

Rhosili
Bay

Hardings
Down

Swansea Bay

Rhosili Downs

Cefn
Reynoldston   Bryn

Clyne Common

Worms
Head

Viel

Parkmill   Kittrough

Bishopston

Oystermouth

Pennrice

Port Eynon Bay

Three Cliffs Bay

Pwlldu Bay

Langland Bay

Mumbles Head

Pavilland
Cave

Oxwich Bay

144